Translated and annotated with historical references by
James Loriega,
Maestro de Armas Blancas Sevillanas, International Masters
at Arms Federation (IMAF).

This translation is dedicated to the handful of
devoted masters of historic edged-weapon disciplines who
individually labor to preserve and proselytize their
Western martial traditions: Ramón Martínez, Jeannette
Acosta-Martínez, Andrea Lupo Sinclair, Paul MacDonald,
Cosimo Bruno, and James Keating.

All of warm hearts and cold steel.

Also by James Loriega:

Sevillian Steel: The Traditional Knife-Fighting Arts of Spain

Manual of the Baratero: *The Art of Handling the* Navaja, *the Knife, and the Scissors of the Gypsies*
Translated by James Loriega

ISBN 13: 978-1-58160-471-9
Printed in the United States of America

Published by Paladin Press, a division of
Paladin Enterprises, Inc.,
Gunbarrel Tech Center
7077 Winchester Circle
Boulder, Colorado 80301 USA
+1.303.443.7250

Direct inquiries and/or orders to the above address.

PALADIN, PALADIN PRESS, and the
are trademarks belonging to Paladin Enterprises and
registered in United States Patent and Trademark Office.

Visit our Web site at www.paladin-press.com

Manual of the Baratero

or
The Art of Handling the Navaja, the Knife, and the Scissors of the Gypsies

Translated by James Loriega
Foreword by Maestro Ramón Martínez

Paladin Press · Boulder, Colorado

Table of Contents

Foreword by Maestro Ramón Martínez vii
Translator's Notes xiii
About the Illustrations xix
Preface: Perspectives on the *Baratero* xxi

PROLOGUE xxxiii

SECTION ONE: INSTRUCTION ON THE *NAVAJA* 1
   First Lesson: Of the *Navaja* 1
   Second Lesson:
      Of the Names by Which the *Navaja* is Known 3
   Third Lesson: Of Positions or Stances 4
   Fourth Lesson:
      Methods for Attacking and Defending Oneself 6
   Fifth Lesson: Of Boundaries 7
   Sixth Lesson: Pivots and How to Make Them 7
   Seventh Lesson: Of Counterpivots 8
   Eighth Lesson: Foists 9
   Ninth Lesson: Of Attacks 13
   Tenth Lesson: Parries, Evasions 15
   Eleventh Lesson: Recourses 17

SECTION TWO: VARIOUS TACTICS PERFORMED
WHEN FIGHTING WITH THE *NAVAJA* **21**
   First Lesson: Guard Positions 21
   Second Lesson: Attacks from the Front 24
   Third Lesson: Attacks from the Flank 25
   Fourth Lesson: *Corridas* 25
   Fifth Lesson: *Molinete* 28
   Sixth Lesson: Throwing the *Navaja* 30
   Seventh Lesson: Movements with the Hat and Hand . 30
   Eighth Lesson: *Recortes* 32

Ninth Lesson: Tactic of the Snake 32
Tenth Lesson: Deceptions 33
Eleventh Lesson: Ruses 34

SECTION THREE: THE PROPER WAY TO HANDLE THE *CUCHILLO* 37
First Lesson: Of the *Cuchillo* 37
Second Lesson: Stances 39
Third Lesson: Attacks; Methods of Throwing the *Puñal* . .40
Fourth Lesson: Evasions and Escapes 40
Fifth Lesson: Recourses and Ruses 40
Sixth Lesson: Defenses against the *Puñal* 40

SECTION FOUR: THE WAY THE GYPSIES HANDLE THE SCISSORS 43
First Lesson: Of the Scissors 43
Second Lesson: Methods of Handling Them 45

THE *BARATERO* 49
Manual del Disparatero 57

AFTERWORD 61

MANUAL DEL BARATERO (reprinted original Spanish version) 63

Appendix A:
The Language of the *Baratero* 113

Appendix B:
The *Baratero*-Based Syllabus 121

Appendix C:
Partial List of Other Works by M.d.R. 125

BIBLIOGRAPHY 127

ABOUT THE TRANSLATOR 131

Foreword

by Maestro Ramón Martínez

Director, Martínez Academy of Arms
President, Association for Historical Fencing
Founding member, International Masters at Arms Federation

Although my profession is that of fencing master, or *maestro de armas,* my early familial instruction in the use of the folding knife contributed to my training as a swordsman. I had a knife in my hand many years before I even touched a sword. In this sense, my childhood experiences were not dissimilar to those of my friend and colleague James Loriega.

When I was a young boy my father always carried a folding knife, and I recall using my own knife two or three times a day to cut the twine off the bundles of clothing that arrived at my father's dry cleaning/tailor shop from the main plant.

Across the street, the stockmen and clerks who worked in the corner *bodega* used their knives to cut up cardboard boxes and string before tying the pieces together to be hauled away by the garbage truck. During lunch breaks they used their knives to peel fruit and to slice bread, *salchichón*, and pieces of cheese.

The most common item used for all these daily tasks was a simple pocketknife, which, as often as not, had a basic locking system to keep it safely open. Contrary to the stereotypical image perpetuated by Broadway and Hollywood in *West Side Story*, the push-button "switchblade" was a luxury item and not at all common in the Puerto Rican community where I grew up. Nor was there any "machismo" glamor associated with carrying a knife—it was seen merely as a tool that served many functions.

A constant companion as well as an ally, the pocketknife was primarily a tool and was only secondarily considered a means of personal protection. In this latter role, the knife was regarded matter-of-factly among the male community. I clearly recall the old men in the neighborhood remarking that the best knife for personal defense was the folding Spanish clasp knife, which they referred to as the *navaja sevillana*. However, since traditional *navajas* were not readily available in New York City, everyone made do with the pocketknives that were.

My father showed me various ways of carrying a knife for easy access in case of sudden need. He also demonstrated how to open it quickly while moving into an offensive posture, enabling one to cut or stab an attacker and then immediately move to a neutral position of safety.

"Never show your knife to anyone," my father admonished, "and only take it out if you or a loved one are threatened with imminent injury from an attacker or robber." He also reminded me that "this situation is a moment of sadness and one to be avoided, as once this step is taken there is no turning back. When a knife is drawn, serious injury, maiming, and death will be the inevitable result." That was the first instruction that I received in the use of the folding knife as a weapon of *personal defense*.

During a visit to Puerto Rico when I was 16, the topic of knives and personal defense came up during a late lunch with my father and uncle. When we finished eating the two men looked at each other and said, "It is time." I was summoned to the garage and handed a knife. My father and uncle proceeded to teach me several ways of using the knife when facing a similarly armed adversary. The instruction was not formal, and the methods taught were intended to end a combat brutally, swiftly, and finally.

The lesson lasted approximately 20 minutes, and in that brief period of time all that I needed to know was imparted to me. My father and uncle explained that, along with the skills I had acquired, the willingness to unemotionally and cold-bloodedly hurt an adversary was imperative.

Today I am internationally known for my reconstruction of *La Verdadera Destreza,* or The True Art and Skill of Spanish Swordsmanship, which is the gentleman's science and art of defense with the rapier. I first became aware of Maestro Loriega when a student who had heard me speak of the *navaja* showed me a copy of *Sevillian Steel,* the first English-language book on Spanish knife fighting. Shortly thereafter, I met Maestro Loriega and was immediately impressed by his incredible range of knowledge and deft skill in handling the *navaja sevillana.*

I demonstrated some of the techniques that I learned as a boy, and Maestro Loriega told me that they were consistent with those originating from southern Spain. It immediately became obvious to us both that I had been taught in a living tradition. The Spanish legacy of fighting with steel had been kept alive in the South Bronx and in Puerto Rico by members of the older generation. I realized how fortunate I was to have a portion of that knowledge passed on to me.

I have subsequently taken classes from Maestro Loriega in order to increase the knowledge that my family had kept for generations and to improve my technical skill. In that time, we have compared the vocabulary and theory of Spanish rapier fencing to the vocabulary and theory of Spanish knife fighting. In doing so, we have found corollaries in the basic principles between both of these indigenous Spanish weapons. A number of these corollaries are also found in the *Manual del Baratero.*

When I was conducting my research into Spanish swordsmanship, the director of one of the libraries I frequented brought an original copy of the *Manual del Baratero* to my attention. I read it but quickly dismissed it because I questioned what it described and depicted. I felt it was not only impractical but could prove downright dangerous to the user who attempted some of the techniques it contained. I determined that there was nothing I could learn from this text that would be of use to me, reasoning that, in any case, one cannot learn how to fight from a book. (I was not aware of the rarity of the copy I had read until I met Maestro Loriega a few years later. That copy of the *Manual del Baratero* had the full name of the author—Mariano de Rementeria y Fica—printed on the cover. This was not the case in other copies of this work, where the author is identified only by the initials M.d.R.)

After my initial meeting with Maestro Loriega, I read the *Manual* again more carefully and came to realize that here was a manual of the *Destreza* for the *common man*. Though extremely brief and superficially written, *Manual del Baratero* is nonetheless the first book on the art of Spanish knife fighting ever published and the only known historical text on the subject. Even though Mariano de Rementeria y Fica may not have had an in-depth knowledge of the methods of the *navaja*, he nonetheless provided for posterity a window to the methods of knife fighting practiced in 19th century Spain by the working class, the *barateros*, and, in particular, the Gypsies.

Since Spanish knife fighting is, for all intents and purposes, unknown outside of Spanish-speaking cultures, its tenets have heretofore been passed down only by word of mouth from generation to generation. For this reason, the present translation of the *Manual del Baratero* is of extreme importance; it introduces the reader—whether Hispanophile, historian, or martial artist—to the *navaja* system that was widely practiced throughout Spain in the 19th century. More significantly, the translation has been prepared by a recognized master of *acero sevillano* and brings unique insider knowledge into the interpretation of the text.

There have been a number of attempts to interpret the manual in the past, but those stilted efforts become glaringly inarticulate in the presence of Maestro Loriega's current translation. I am aware of no one who is better qualified to present as comprehensive a translation as is provided here. Maestro Loriega brings to the work an intimate understanding of Spanish language, history, culture, and tradition; a technical mastery of regional *navaja* styles; and an innate ability to explain the manual's content within the larger context of the edged weapons arts practiced throughout the world.

In point of fact, many of James' personal comments also lend perspective to our appreciation of Central and South American edged-weapons combat. Spanish colonizing efforts were more widespread south of our borders, and we can still see how the techniques of the *navaja* and *cuchillo* influenced the edged-weapon methods of Argentinean *gauchos* and Mexican *vaqueros*, who are renown for their knife-and-poncho styles of fighting. With this work, James reveals the correlation between the Andalusian knife arts and the knife arts that have evolved throughout the Americas.

In the end, I believe that the art of skillfully wielding the *navaja* is in fact a noteworthy type of fencing, one that has never received the attention that it rightly deserved until now. I am proud to have contributed in a small way toward the appearance of this often-misunderstood manual, and happy that it is at last within reach of Western martial arts scholars and practitioners. I commend Maestro Loriega for this painstaking and meticulous translation and predict that his work will enrich the understanding of bladed personal combat for all those who practice the arts of the knife and sword. The legacy of Spanish steel lives on. *Dios, corrazon y acero!*

Translator's Notes

In recent years we have witnessed a resurgence of interest in the diverse body of combat systems collectively referred to as Western martial arts. The current level of awareness extends far beyond the familiar arts of boxing, wrestling, and savate to such unique and specialized disciplines as Viking sword, Irish cudgel, German *dussack*, French smallsword, Italian rapier, Sicilian stiletto, and Spanish *navaja*.

The publisher of this manual, characteristically responsive to the pulse of the martial arts public (Western as well as Eastern), has acted expeditiously to fill the technical and informational void created by this modern interest in ancient methods. In short time Paladin Press has added a comprehensive selection of technical manuals, scholarly treatises, and contemporary translations of rare and historic texts to its already extensive list of publications. It was in keeping with its goal of providing readers with the best source material available that Paladin Press commissioned the present translation of *Manual del Baratero*.

Manual del Baratero was first published anonymously in 1849 in Madrid by the publishing house of Alberto Goya. Despite the fact that its author was merely identified as "M.d.R.," the work has the distinction of being the oldest dedicated manual on the subject of knife fighting.

I first became aware of the *Manual del Baratero* in 1975. It was given a passing mention in William Cassidy's *Complete Book of Knife Fighting* (which I had just received as part of my first book order from Paladin). At that time, the manual had been in existence for more than 125 years.

In the years that followed, I encountered other references to the manual but never much information about it. I began to wonder whether the manual actually existed or if the writers who cited it were merely taking their cue from Cassidy's book. Though I continued finding references to it, the actual manual persisted in eluding me for nearly 20 years. It was not until I approached Rafael Martínez del Peral, Esq., the Madrid-based *navaja* collector and author of *La Navaja Española Antigua*, that I finally obtained a copy of the often-cited but rarely seen text.

Manual del Baratero turned out to be a very fascinating book, not so much for its instructional content but for the glimpse it provided into a segment of Spanish society from an age gone by. To be certain, its technical content is elementary, its descriptions superficial, and its scope limited and uneven. Yet the manual's Prologue, along with its end essay on the phenomenon of the *baratero*—a denizen of the underworld described in the Preface—affords the reader firsthand historical and sociological insights into the era. Class rivalries, social values, gender roles, criminal behaviors, and other aspects of mid-19th-century Spain are portrayed in the author's detailed, if at times ineloquent, descriptions.

On a personal level, the manual also lent perspective to many of the terms and phrases I had often heard but never understood. (I have an aunt, for example, who is fond of warning, "*Te vas a buscar un santólio*"[1] whenever she's cautioning me against doing something she considers dangerous. She does not know what a *santólio* is, but from hearing it all her life she knows that it forebodes a serious problem. The manual showed me that a *santólio* is a very large *navaja,* or traditional Spanish clasp-knife characterized by the clasp or ring to lock or release the blade and fold it into the handle. Thus, looking to find one, as my aunt warns, is tantamount to looking for trouble.)

Since, apart from its archaic words, I was readily able to read and comprehend the contents of the manual, I never felt the need to translate it into English. In the mid-1990s, however, the late Don Santiago Rivera proposed that I undertake its translation. Don Santiago was a *maestro de armas blancas,* or master of edged weapons, who maintained a small but well-known "*navaja* school" in Seville's Barrio Santa Cruz. It was from this *maestro* that I received my first formal instruction in *acero sevillano,*[2] which was the personal term he used to describe his edged-weapons arts.

Santiago felt that the translation would fulfill a dual purpose: to serve as my "thesis" for instructorship in *acero sevillano* and to help present a small component of Spain's historic martial culture to the non-Spanish-speaking world.

In 1996 I translated the manual, received my instructorship, and circulated the rough translation among the few who expressed interest in the Spanish knife arts. Other than that, the translation has occupied shelf space in my training hall alongside many others of its kind.

During the recent process of refining my old translation, I came to appreciate the modern translator's quandary in deciding whether to remain faithful to the letter of an original work or be true to the spirit of its meaning. Had the manual been a classic piece of literature, I might have opted to be faithful to it to the letter. However, since it was an instructional work, I decided to instead be true to its intent. That notwithstanding, I endeavored to adhere to the manual's choice of words and phrases as closely as possible while sparing the reader from becoming entangled in idiomatic expressions that have no literal meaning in English.

Throughout the translation process I was challenged by many of the conventions of the Spanish language as it was written more than a century and a half ago. Chief among these challenges was the fact that many of the words and terms that appeared in the manual are unused in the spoken Spanish of today. Related to this was the fact that some of the words found in the manual have completely different meanings today.[3]

A second challenge came in the form of inordinately long sentences that were commonly found in 19th century writings (as prevalent in English works as they were in Spanish). The final challenge came from the author's discrepancies and literary inconsistencies throughout the manual.

To overcome the first and most difficult challenge, I had to consult individuals who, whether by vocation or avocation, were familiar with the edged-weapons lexicon of 19th century Spain. I was fortunate to find Ignacio Morales in Seville, Francisco Abellan Martínez in Madrid, and Maestro Ramón Martínez in the United States considerate of my plight and extremely helpful with their individual insights. Each of these men is conversant not only in the Spanish language but also, of equal significance, in the practical use of Spanish edged weapons and of the terms—common and uncommon—related to them.

I resolved the issue of inordinately long sentences by editing the manual's extended clauses in a manner that was more cohesive and compatible with today's style of writing. This required extensive changes in punctuation as well as added words to enhance clarity and maintain coherence. I went to great lengths to ensure that the meaning and context of the rephrasing remained faithful to the original text.

I dealt with the challenge posed by the author's discrepancies by simply highlighting them with footnotes, thus allowing the reader to come to his or her own conclusions as to M.d.R.'s intentions.

As much to maintain the manual's historical flavor as to avoid losing the ineffable "something" that inevitably gets lost in translations, I kept a number of the terms in the original

Spanish. I did this as much with contemporary terms like *navaja*, *cuchillo*, and *puñal* as with many of the obsolete terms, such as *molinete*, *corridas*, and *recortes*.

Although not originally undertaken with publication in mind, I believe this translation to be a responsibly accurate one—so much so that even Spanish-fluent readers should have little trouble with my particular choices of words and turns of phrases. It is thus my sincere hope that Western martial arts aficionados, as well as edged-weapons enthusiasts of all persuasions, derive new insights from my admittedly personal interpretation of this long-lost manual—one that has not been readily available since its initial publication more than 150 years ago.

NOTES

1. "You're looking to find yourself a *santólio*."
2. Sevillian steel; the informal name used to denote the knife-fighting systems of Andalusia.
3. The primary source used for technical definitions was the *Collins Diccionario Español-Inglés, Inglés-Español*, 5th ed., 1999.

About the Illustrations

Although we know the identity of the erstwhile anonymous author of the *Manual del Baratero*, nothing is known about the artist who illustrated it. Throughout the world there exist less than a handful of publicly accessible editions of the *original* manual. In the United States, one original is archived in New York City's Mid-Manhattan Library and another at the Hispanic Society of America, while facsimiles are available at the Library of Congress. The artist's identity, however, is not clear from either copy.

Because of the poor-quality drawings that are found in the available facsimiles of the manual, I thought it fitting to complement them with sharper and better-preserved illustrations by 19th century artists José Luís Pellicer (Spain) and Gustave Doré (France). Pellicer's illustration, *Los Barateros*, originally accompanied an article of the same name, written by Mariano José de Larra. Both the illustration and the article appeared in *El Español*, a Madrid-based daily, on April 19, 1836. Doré's illustrations are from *Spain*, originally published in Paris as *L'Espagne* in 1862.

Doré, of course, was one of the most popular and accomplished illustrators of all time, establishing his reputation with works of art that embodied Romantic style, abundant details, and a dramatic use of light and shade. Throughout the 1860s and 1870s he undertook an extended journey through Spain accompanied by his friend, Baron Jean-Charles Davillier. Davillier, an art scholar, writer, and experienced Spanish traveler, had arranged to document their travels for the French publisher Hachette. Doré illustrated the travelogue, and it is from this popular collaboration, *Spain*, that many of the *navajero* and *baratero* illustrations in the present translation were taken.

Some have speculated that Doré (1832–1883) was also the illustrator of *Manual del Baratero*. Others propose that he illustrated a later European edition. Such speculation is born of familiarity with his work depicting *navajeros* and *barateros* during the latter part of his prolific career, yet even the most inexperienced eye will agree that the drawings in the manual do not portray the detail and fluid anatomy that, in part, characterize Doré's inimitable style. All we know for certain is that some of Doré's illustrations were also added to a leatherbound reprint published in Spain in 1994.

In addition to the illustrations from his own travelogue, Doré drew many other Spanish-themed illustrations for both Prosper Mérimée's *Carmen* and Théophile Gautier's *Captain Fracasse*. The interested reader should note that these two examples of French Romantic fiction include copious descriptions of *navaja* combat.

Though he lived only to age 51, the sheer bulk of Doré's work is mind-boggling in scope. Thanks to his prolific abilities as an artist, this and future generations can enjoy a glimpse of *barateros, navajas,* knife fighting, and other scenes typical of Spanish life in the 19th century—a time when everyone knew what a *baratero* was, and when everyone had his own *navaja*.

Preface
Perspectives on the *Baratero*

Weigh matters carefully, and think hardest about those that matter most. All fools come to grief from lack of thought. They never conceive even the half of things, and because they do not perceive either their advantages or their harm, they do not apply any diligence. Some ponder things backward, paying much attention to what matters little, and little to what matters much. Many people never lose their heads because they have none to lose. There are things we should consider very carefully and keep well rooted in our minds. The wise weigh everything: they delve into things that are especially deep or doubtful, and sometimes reflect that there is more than what occurs to them. Thus they make comprehension reach further than apprehension.

—Baltasar Gracián
Aphorism 35, *The Art of Worldly Wisdom*

The many chapters in *Manual del Baratero* comprise an album of snapshots that help depict the ways in which *armas blancas cortas*, or small edged weapons, were used on the dark and grimy cobblestone streets of 19th century Spain. Yet, just as photographs can be misinterpreted when viewed out of context, so too can the lessons contained in *Manual del Baratero* when one lacks a proper understanding of the era and society for which they were written.

Before we delve into the contents of the manual or attempt to understand the methods described therein, we must first gain an understanding, albeit a cursory one, of the Spanish criminal subculture of the time. It was, after all, the members of this subculture who used small edged weapons with regularity, just as it was the existence of this subculture that made skill with such weapons a necessity—as much for the criminals who used it to pursue their livelihoods as for those of the other classes who used it to preserve their lives.

The requisite insight into the criminal subculture of Spain's past can be gained by looking at what society was like in Seville. Seville was a microcosm of Spain, and although *Manual del Baratero* was published in Madrid, Spain's capital city was hardly the only venue where the arts of the *navaja* were practiced. Far from it. Those arts had always been ascribed to Spain's southernmost cities and towns in Andalusia, among them Córdoba, Granada, Cádiz, Jaén, Ronda, Málaga, and Seville.

The use of the *navaja* was so commonplace in Seville that, among the old-time Spaniards skilled in its use, one of the most customary terms for the knife was *sevillana*.[1] This is a clear indication of the degree to which the weapon, in its most lethal configuration, was a familiar accoutrement throughout the province of Seville and indeed of all Andalusia.

Of course, not everyone agreed that Andalusia's capital city was also the capital of *navaja* expertise. Davillier, for example, held a different opinion. In *Spain*, a classic 19th century travelogue for which he supplied the narrative and Gustave Doré the illustrations, Davillier writes,

> If the use of the *navaja*, the *puñal*, and the *cuchillo*, is general in Spain, there are certain towns where the "wholesome traditions" are carefully preserved. Córdoba and Seville possess very famous fencing-masters, but nowhere is the art of handling cold steel, the *herramienta*, cultivated to so great an extent as at Málaga. Few towns show such a leaning towards homicide; *delitos de sangre*—crimes of blood—are extremely frequent.

Nonetheless, Davillier is willing to concede that Sevillian *barateros* are ranked, in his opinion, a close second to the Málagueños. He writes, "After those of Málaga, the *barateros* of Seville are the most dangerous of all Andalusia, and they practice their hideous work in the same manner."

Yet, whether speaking of Málaga or Seville, Barcelona or

Madrid, few historians will argue that the *barateros* from these cities were among those most predisposed to wielding a *navaja*—for little reason or none—in the backstreets, beaches, and prisons of Spain.

THE WORLD OF THE *BARATERO*

The world of the *baratero* was in fact the underworld, thickly populated by scoundrels, ruffians, prostitutes, beggars, thieves, and assassins for hire. In Spain, this entire underclass was referred to as *vagabundos* (vagabonds), a pejorative reserved for any able-bodied person who shunned respectable jobs.[2] The *vagabundos* not only belonged to the same underworld but also used a language unique to themselves, known as *germania* (pronounced her-MAHN-ya).[3]

"[This] thieves' jargon," notes Ruth Pike, a historian and author on early modern Seville, "was used in common speech throughout the city, [where] everyone went about armed for protection." It is from *germania* that many of the terms found in the manual originate.

The criminal subculture, also known as *la gente del hampa* (pronounced AHM-pa)[4] was not specific to the 19th century but had roots as far back as the 16th century. Describing Seville in that era, Pike writes,

> Such a city, overflowing with wealth, vice, and poverty, presented the most favorable conditions for the shelter and protection of vagrants and lawbreakers of every sort. With a large population and an exceedingly lax and corrupt municipal government, the town was filled with all types of disreputable elements. . . . Criminals could usually escape the law by moving from one district to another or even by fleeing to the Indies.

This is hardly surprising when one realizes that, as historian Mary Elizabeth Perry notes in *Crime and Society in Early Modern Seville*, Andalusia's capital was really two cities:

It was the city of an oligarchy that included land-owning nobles, wealthy merchants, and leaders of the Church. It was also the city of an underworld that retained an identity separate from the dominant culture. . . . Any study of crime and society in Seville must begin with a discussion of these two groups.

The most notorious of the districts where *la gente del hampa* resided was Triana, the name given to Seville's *gitaneria*. The *gitaneria*, or gypsy quarter, was at once the home to the bravest of bullfighters and the most brazen of criminals. English missionary George Borrow described the district as follows:

> The faubourg of Triana, in Seville, has from time immemorial been noted as a favourite residence of the *Gitanos*; and here, at the present day, they are to be found in greater number than in any other town in Spain. This faubourg is indeed chiefly inhabited by desperate characters, as, besides the *Gitanos*, the principal part of the robber population of Seville is here congregated. Perhaps there is no part even of Naples where crime so much abounds, and the law is so little respected, as at Triana, the character of whose inmates was so graphically delineated two centuries and a half back by Cervantes, in one of the most amusing of his tales.

Pike paints us a colorful picture of these "desperate characters" and further distinguishes the two principal factions of what she kindly calls "disreputable elements" as vagrants and beggars on the one hand and professional criminals (thieves, enforcers, murderers) on the other. The *baratero* belonged to the latter group, which also included rogues (*pícaros*), ruffians (*jácaros*), and bullies (*rufos*). At their lowest level these criminals were nothing more than thugs and assassins. "Their principal activities," explains Pike, "consisted of inflicting punishment for pay—murders, stabbings, cudgelings, ink throwings, and the nailing of horns over the doors of cuckolds." As we shall see, inflicting punishment for pay was an integral part of the *baratero's* job description.

THE *BARATERO*

To better understand the *baratero's* role and function, we must understand gambling as a Spanish vice. Writing of Spain during its Golden Age, French historian Marcelin Defourneaux notes,

> The passion for gaming, which ravaged every class, was a sure source of revenue for those who knew how to exploit it. Authorized gaming-houses were in existence . . . but far more numerous were the gambling-houses (*garitos*) where professional gamblers lay in wait to fleece too gullible clients. Sometimes they formed themselves into groups, in which each member of the gang had a special job.

Among the members of such gangs, there were the *fullero*, or card sharp, who prepared various decks of marked cards; the *jácaro*, who was poised to disappear with the money; and the *pregonero*, or tout, who was charged with finding and drawing unsuspecting gamblers to the game. When the tout's duties also included enforcing wagers or collecting a percentage of the winnings, he was considered a *baratero*.

No exact translation exists for *baratero* in English. *The Dictionary of the Royal Academy of the Spanish Language* informs us that it was "one who by one means or another exacted the 'barato' from the winnings of gamblers." *Barato*, in this sense, means a percentage of the winnings. "By one means or another" is significant here.

While his specific tasks might have varied from one region of Spain to another—and from one type of game to another—the *baratero's* general role was essentially that of a facilitator to gamblers. Apart from the illegal *garitos*, his domain was an alley, side street, or cul-de-sac hidden from the eyes of the *guardia civil* (local police) and decent citizens. At times, this would actually be in the back shadows of the cities' churches and cathedrals. As Perry observes,

> In los Olmos and los Naranjos, two patios immediately next to the Cathedral, a scruffier group of people congregated. Many were beggars, and a few carried secondhand clothing or fruits and vegetables, which they hawked in the streets. Most had a knife or other weapon; some carried marked cards and loaded dice.

THE TOOLS OF THE *BARATERO*

The items listed in Perry's last sentence are, of course, the classic tools of the *baratero's* trade. Interestingly, one of the more popular slang terms for *navaja* was *herramienta*, which literally means "[iron] tool." Should a gambler—whether winner or loser—decline paying his *barato* to the *baratero*, he would invariably find himself pleading his case before the sharp point of an unforgiving *navaja*. This understandably contributed to the association of the *navaja* with the members of the underworld. In *Daggers and Fighting Knives of the Western World*, Harold C. Peterson opines, "Spaniards of the lower classes were evidently resourceful in their choice of weapons."

But Peterson tends to overgeneralize. In Spain, the carrying of a *navaja* did not necessarily identify the individual as a criminal. Possession of the clasp-knife was left to the discretion of each citizen. Actually, the *navaja* enjoyed a mainstream acceptance that extended across Spain's social classes, as Arturo Sanchez de Vivar, author of the colorfully illustrated *La Navaja Clásica*, clearly illustrates:

> In his book titled *Manual del Baratero o Arte de Manejar Bien la Navaja*[6] [sic], M.d.R. tells us: "The *navaja*, in essence, is the personal weapon, as we have already said, of the working class, of the mule-driver, of

the transporter, of the artisan, of the sailor, and so indispensable a tool that many cannot afford to be without it."

But it would not be destined for only this social class for too long. Step by step, its manufacture grew and there came to light more and better-skilled artisans who brought the *navaja* to greater heights, enhancing it through better and finer materials, and establishing its true place as an edged weapon.

Little by little, the *navaja* became more accepted, appreciated, and used by all the social classes of Spanish society; not only the working class, but the middle class and aristocracy soon adopted *navajas* as their inseparable companions. Evidence of this rests in the fact that many of the original samples found today in museum collections reflect a standard of materials and craftsmanship that could only have been afforded by the upper classes.

That was in fact the case. Some 50 years after the publication of *Manual del Baratero*, Sevillians were still carrying *navajas* as a matter of course. In *The Story of Seville*, written as part of the *Medieval Towns* series at the turn of the last century, British author Walter M. Gallichan writes, "Most of the working class carry the *navaja*, a knife with a long blade, a sharp edge, and a keen point." He further clarifies that "The *navaja* is never worn or used ostentatiously."

Gallichan's observation also invalidates another one of Peterson's unfounded speculations in *Daggers and Fighting Knives*: "The *navaja* may well have continued in use until 1900 or later, at least in remote parts of the Iberian Peninsula, but it certainly had lost its popularity well before that time. Thus one may safely assume that this was primarily a nineteenth-century knife."

In actuality, the *navaja*'s quotidian use was never limited to "remote parts" of Iberia. Moreover, its popularity as an accoutrement of the populace has survived to the present; thus, for those who carry it, the *navaja* is, as is any other, a knife of the 21st century.

THE "ART" OF THE *BARATERO*

Returning to the subject of the *baratero* and his contemporaries, Pike tells us that, in addition to sharing a mutual language and a common desire to live without working, the *gente del hampa* freely borrowed each other's tricks. Such tricks ran the gamut from subtle swindles to duplicitous knife attacks. As an example, Pike cites a special knife thrust invented by one Gayón, an infamous criminal whose technique became regarded as indispensable by street toughs. (Regrettably, Pike does not describe the technique.)

We would not be wrong in assuming that many of the *engaños* (deceptions), *suertes* (tactics), and *tretas* (feints) cataloged in *Manual del Baratero* began as "tricks" used by the criminal subculture. While many of these so-called tricks seem unsophisticated by today's standards, bear in mind that we have the benefit of 15 decades of tactical evolution.

Furthermore, despite the seeming artlessness of the *engaños*, *suertes*, and *tretas*, taken together they nonetheless constitute an *art*, rudimentary as it may be, of knife fighting—and more so when one adds the street strategies and underdog philosophies of those who employed the methods almost daily. Viewed as a whole, then, the combined tricks, tactics, strategies, and combat attitudes formed the art—no less for being a "street art"—of the *baratero*. It was this art, used not only by *barateros* but also by assorted other denizens of the *hampa*, that was recorded and depicted by the author of the manual.

THE AUTHOR OF *MANUAL DEL BARATERO*

For many years, the identity of the mysterious M.d.R. baffled many American enthusiasts in the Western martial arts. I specify *American* because the initials M.d.R. ring familiar to

European bibliophiles and collectors of treatises and manuals. Mariano de Rementeria y Fica, the actual author of *Manual del Baratero*, was a prolific 19th century researcher, translator, and writer of manuals. From the titles of his works, we can infer that, apart from being fluent in French and Italian, Mariano was probably the classic anal-retentive personality, as said titles demonstrate a clear affinity for subjects that lend themselves to listing, classifying, and structuring. (A partial listing of other works written or translated by Mariano de Rementeria appears in Appendix C.)

For all of his empirical knowledge, however, Mariano seems to have lacked the courage of his convictions—at least where *Manual del Baratero* was concerned. Why else would he have affixed his full name to numerous manuals related to Spanish grammar, French cooking, and male grooming but only his initials to his primer on knife fighting? Did he not believe in earnest the many concepts he promotes in his Prologue? Probably not.

More than likely Mariano was a researcher with a compulsion to categorize and record every body of knowledge he came across or in which he felt there was public interest. He may have been a grammarian, but he was in all likelihood not a cook, not a pastry chef, and certainly not an expert in the art of knife fighting. In fact, as a member of the same "so-called decent society" against whom he railed, Mariano could not afford to have his name connected with the ignoble *barateros*. Had the manual been properly attributed to him, he stood to lose his respectable standing among academicians and food connoisseurs.

Given the probability of Mariano's dilettante status, the techniques and tactics reflected in the manual were not only incomplete but also of a clearly superficial nature. Furthermore, some of the methods he included are downright fanciful and unrelated to the practical and sober maneuvers that characterize true Spanish knife fighting. The Third Lesson in Section One ("Of Positions or Stances") is a good example: no skilled knife fighter would stand fully facing an opponent, exposing a major number of vulnerable targets to attack. Similarly, the "Tactic of the

Snake," like the advice to unravel the sash and wait for the opponent to step on it, is comedic in its strategic naiveté.

In truth, however, the practicality of the techniques matters little, for, as I explain in *Sevillian Steel: The Traditional Knife-Fighting Arts of Spain* (Paladin Press, 1999), Mariano's purpose in naming his work *Manual del Baratero* was to emphasize the fact that those of the lower classes were better equipped to defend themselves than those of the upper classes. In essence, if the working-class man was to learn how to defend himself adequately, he was better served by following the example of those below him than of those above. That is not to say, however, that the manual is successful in providing the necessary instruction.

Regretably for the numerous Western martial artists who have sought to reconstruct a historic knife-fighting system from it, the sad fact is that *Manual del Baratero* does not provide a practical system of combat. While some of the notions it contains are indeed those used in the Spanish knife arts, the majority of the techniques and tactics it contains are inaccurate, unfeasible, or impractical, and otherwise misrepresented.

Yet, though the actual techniques set down by Mariano appear to be of little use today, the topics he focused on represent important aspects of combat that are as relevant now as they were when the manual was written. In point of fact, there are many *navaja* devotees who use the list of chapter topics as a yardstick by which to measure the completeness of their own *personal* methods. Though the techniques of the *baratero* represent the most basic of *navaja* techniques, they serve as a valid starting point for understanding the core of the art of knife fighting. An example of how to do this is presented in Appendix B.

THE MANUAL'S MOST IMPORTANT LESSON

The reader is encouraged to read the manual with an open mind, devoid of preconceptions. Ultimately, if there is one valid lesson that can be internalized from reading *Manual del Baratero*—one not found in the book—it is to never lose sight of the prime objective in knife combat: *survival.* By keeping this objective foremost in mind, one will do whatever is needed—whether it be attacks, counters, recourses, ruses, or deceptions—to overcome to the threat of an edged weapon.

ACKNOWLEDGMENTS

My sincere appreciation goes out to the following individuals for their support in the reincarnation of this manual: Antone Blair, Pete Kautz, Jared Kirby, Ken Pfrenger, Lane Powers, Evan Stachowiak, and Karin Taylor.

—James Loriega

NOTES

1. A *navaja* with formidable point and edge qualities, specifically designed for combat. Such *navajas* were called *sevillanas* because Seville was believed to be the city where such knives were most frequently and expertly used. *Sevillanas* are typically characterized by a ratcheted locking mechanism, long and slender blade, needle-sharp point, and finely honed edge.
2. Vagabonds. Members of the criminal underclass.
3. Language of the criminal underworld; thieves' slang. The term is derived from *hermandad,* which means "brotherhood;" in this particular case, a brotherhood of thieves.
4. The underworld; the criminal classes.
5. The error in the title of the manual is copied from Sanchez' book.

Prologue

There will perhaps be those who, upon seeing the present manual, will view it as reprehensible, assuming its existence to be detrimental due to the fact that the *navaja* is the personal weapon of *barateros*, of gamblers, and of certain other individuals of the wrathful life—individuals whom it is better they avoid than [have] to learn precepts that will result in injury to oneself and, consequently, to society.

To those who would say thus, we reply by pointing out that when there exist in this society certain irre-

The Gipsy Boy

mediable ills for which the precepts of religion are not sufficient—nor the most sublime moral treatises, nor laws, nor the
most efficient measures—it behooves us to adopt a method
that makes said ills less cruel; that is, to train such honorable
and peaceful men as might find themselves unjustly attacked
by those who are skilled in the use of weapons and who, pro-
tected by this advantage, resort to insults or aggression at the
slightest word or deed, or for the mere pleasure of doing harm.

Spain has enacted stringent laws against dueling, attempting to eradicate this barbarous custom bequeathed to us from
chivalrous times. Yet, nothing has been achieved. Every day, we
witness the resorting to engagements in so-called honorable
combat by the very men charged with the enforcement of the
many decrees, orders, and ordinances that prohibit it.

It is not enough that there are intelligent and virtuous people
who rise up against dueling challenges,[1] calling them the
recourse of dishonest and immoral men. In vain have other countries, more enlightened than our own, formed respectable asso-
ciations for the purpose of ending them [challenges], using all the
recourses governed by an untainted love for humanity. But the
dueling continues; and we have seen, scandalously, not long ago
that the laws are disparaged by the very people who enact them.

"Let us beware," said Rousseau[2] when speaking against
dueling,

> of confusing the sacred name of honor with this fierce
> obsession that places all the virtues at the point of a
> sword; and which serves only to make valiant people
> infamous. What does this obsession entail? The most
> extravagant and barbaric opinion that has ever entered
> the human spirit!
>
> [It purports] that society's responsibilities are satisfied
> with valor; that man is not sly, or roguish, or slanderous,
> but is, on the contrary, correct, courteous, well educat-
> ed, and humane when he knows how to fight; that the
> lie is converted into truth, and honor to deceit; and that

infidelity is made laudable the moment it justifies itself with steel in hand; that an affront is remedied forever by means of a thrust; and that an injustice is never committed against a man for the purpose of killing him.[3]

We see here just a small portion of what has been said against dueling; yet, in spite of everything, there is no lack today of writers who publish treatises that apologetically defend it without caring that their doctrines are in opposition to our laws. What does this show us? The inadequacy of such laws, and the triumph of the duelists' doctrines!

[Given that] dueling challenges are tolerated, teaching the art of handling weapons becomes necessary so that the consequences of the challenge are reduced. There is a need to instruct the weak [man] so that he will know how to defend himself from the boldness of the strong. From times long past there have been men who carry the pompous title of *Maestro mayor de los reinos*; others that are called *Segundos tenientes*, and finally those simply named *Maestros de armas*,[4] who refer to the collection of their precepts as *the most noble art of fencing*.

Those masters of fencing, or *destreza*,[5] as the art was called in ancient times, establish their training halls even in the most public of places, and conduct their lessons in them without the authorities—the protectors of the lives of [our] citizens—disrupting their instructorships, from which nothing good can come but sheer homicides.

And note here the contradiction between one law that prohibits dueling challenges and another that authorizes or sanctions the public tutors of the sword.[6] What else can those [fencing] assaults be, performed no less by persons of the feminine sex, if not schools whose masters teach how to achieve success [by means of spilling] human blood? What does the so-called Lady Castellanos purport to be doing in sessions with the sword? Learning how to kill. Why is the teaching of pistol shooting permissible? Because there are occasions where their use is expedient to self-defense. Thus, even while recognizing that it is an atrocious evil, the dueling challenge must be tolerated, and [therefore] it is advantageous to learn how to fight.

No one is outraged or rises up against a fencing treatise, nor against its precepts. On the contrary, it is regarded as part of the fine education of our upper classes; and one is not fully a gentleman unless he knows how to grip a foil or deliver saber blows. If all this is true, we see no reason why anyone should look upon the teaching of the *navaja* with disdain; moreover we propose to impart those precepts to honorable men so they know how to wield it as a defensive weapon.

It is indubitable that certain people would be less fearful of the *navaja* if they knew how to stop its blows; and proof of this is that when two individuals challenge each other with foils—if both understand its use—the confrontation rarely brings about lethal consequences.

The *navaja* is a weapon generally used in Spain by the working class, and so we are astounded by the aversion with which those of the upper classes view it. Therefore, learn to use [the *navaja*] for certain occasions in the same way you learn to use all other weapons and you will come to appreciate the value of our Manual.

If you respond that it is the weapon with which *barateros* impose the law in the gambling dens and forcefully extract a commission from gamblers, then we should say that it is also [the weapon] of the honorable and peaceful man who finds himself attacked by a pickpocket or thief, and who has no method of defense other than it [the *navaja*] and his heart.

The *navaja*, in essence, is the personal weapon, as we have already said, of the working class, of the mule-driver, of the transporter, of the artisan, of the sailor, and so indispensable a tool that many cannot [afford to] be without it. In view of this, we will set down the necessary rules for its optimal handling in instances that [involve one's] dignity.

Furthermore, [while] there are those who write special treatises on fencing and the use of all gentlemen's arms for [the benefit of] nobles and boorish men with white gloves, we write for the populace, for the townsmen, for those of rough and calloused hands whom gentlemen call *riffraff*, but without whom [the same gentlemen] would be worthless. We write for the townsmen because they also face challenges [that are] almost always more unexpected, more abrupt, and without the benefit of seconds, or witnesses, or the other trifling and fussing found in the duels of aristocrats and of so-called decent people.

Finally, we also write this manual in case our knowledge can be of value to those professional swordsmen who, though perfumed and dressed in fine clothes, are very far from possessing better conduct or morality than men with jackets and sticks, and who are often more deserving of punishment than the heroes of the gambling dens, among whom it is not rare to discover particular traits that are at odds with their dishonest and struggling lives.

M.d.R.

INSTRUCTION FOR HANDLING THE *NAVAJA*

The instructions for handling the *navaja* are divided into four sections.[7]

The first consists of the mechanism of the weapon and of its different positions.

In the second, the guard positions are examined and the way to attack an opponent is explained, giving a brief idea of the various tactics and ruses that can be used.

In the third, the proper way of handling the *cuchillo* is shown.

Finally, in the fourth, the way the scissors are handled among the Gypsies is shown.

The first section is divided into eleven lessons; the second into twelve,[8] the third into six, and the fourth into two, in the following manner:

FIRST SECTION
Instruction on the *Navaja*
First lesson: Of the *Navaja*
Second lesson: Its Most Common Names[9]

Third lesson: Positions or Stances
Fourth lesson: Methods of Attacking and Defending Oneself
Fifth lesson: Of Boundaries
Sixth lesson: Of Turns and How to Make Them
Seventh lesson: Of Counterpivots
Eighth lesson: Foists
Ninth lesson: Of Attacks
Tenth lesson: Of Parries and Evasions
Eleventh lesson: Of the Recourses

SECOND SECTION
Of the Various Tactics Performed Using the *Navaja*
First lesson: Guard Positions
Second lesson: Attacks from the Front
Third lesson: Attacks from the Flank
Fourth lesson: Passes
Fifth lesson: *Molinete*
Sixth lesson: Throwing the *Navaja*
Seventh lesson: Movements of the Hand and the Hat
Eighth lesson: *Recortes*
Ninth lesson: Tactic of the Snake
Tenth lesson: Deceptions
Eleventh lesson: Ruses

THIRD SECTION
The Proper Way of Handling the *Cuchillo*
First lesson: Of the *Cuchillo*
Second lesson: Stances
Third lesson: Attacks; Method of Throwing the *Puñal*
Fourth lesson: Evasions and Escapes
Fifth lesson: Recourses and Ruses
Sixth lesson: Defenses Against the *Cuchillo* or *Puñal*

FOURTH SECTION
The Way of Handling of the Scissors Among the Gypsies
First lesson: Of the Scissors
Second lesson: Gypsies' Methods of Handling Them

NOTES

1. In the manual, *desafios*, which means "challenges." I have taken the liberty of specifying *dueling* challenges, since this was what the author was referring to.
2. Jean-Jacques Rousseau (1712–1778). French philosopher and one of the most important political writers of 18th century France.
3. The author excerpted this quote from Rousseau's romantic novel *La Nouvelle Héloise*.
4. These represent three of the many inflated titles assumed by those who purported to be fencing masters.
5. Dexterity, skill, or adeptness. Spanish fencing was traditionally referred to as *el arte de la Destreza*.
6. In the manual, *florete*, which means a fencing foil. I have substituted "sword" because the author's concerns are with actual dueling as opposed to sport fencing.
7. The original word here is *parte*, which would be "part" in English. I have substituted "section" to distinguish it from other connotations of *parte* that appear later in the manual.
8. Strangely, only 11 are in the manual.
9. In the original Spanish manual, there were minor inconsistencies between the way M.d.R. listed the sections and lessons in his outline of the book's contents in the Prologue and the way they actually appeared in the body of the text. In the interest of historical accuracy, those inconsistencies were retained here. In the new Table of Contents added by the publisher (p. v–vi), section and chapter titles are listed exactly as they appeared in the body of the original text.

Instruction on the *Navaja*

FIRST LESSON
OF THE *NAVAJA*

Given that the *navaja* is a very well-known weapon in our country, we will not tire our readers with a detailed explanation of its simple mechanism. It is enough to know that they come in different sizes, and that not all of them are suited to our purposes.

In Spain there are many towns that are recognized for the good quality and temper with which they imbue the blades of their *navajas*.

La Navaja, by Gustave Doré.

Their sharp edges are such that they are greatly admired for neither breaking nor bending after having pierced two solid peso coins or a board two inches thick. Albacete, Santa Cruz de Mudela, Guadij, Solana, Mora, Bonilla, Valencia, Sevilla, Jaén, and many other places have master blacksmiths by whose hands are wrought works that are better rendered in this industry than can be forged outside our country, and which we recommend to aficionados.

But since the shape of every *navaja* is not always adequate for the use to which we will put it in the course of this instruction, we will say that the blade should at most be one *palmo*[1] in length and be perfectly secured within its handle. This makes a *navaja* with a backspring preferable to any other.

The shape of the blade is of particular interest, since it is not with just any blade that the *diestro*[2] will indiscriminately risk delivering his attacks. Therefore, the blade selected will have a wide belly toward the point, with three or four fingers in width and with a somewhat elongated point capable of delivering *floretazos*,[3] everything as depicted in the accompanying illustration.

Translator's comment:

The use of the word *muelle*, or spring, in the last line of the third paragraph has invariably led some translators to conclude that this refers to a switchblade-like *navaja*. In fact, what the author is referring to here is merely the common backspring found on all modern folding knives. His previous statement that a *navaja* should "be perfectly secured within its handle" supports this.

The backspring that we currently take for granted was not always available in folding knives of past centuries. In *Identifying Pocket Knives*, author and knife collector Bernard Levine reminds us that "the earliest known folding knives had no backsprings in their handles. . . . Although the idea of a spring-back knife seems to be older, reliable spring steel was a product of the mid-18th century—1742 to be exact."

Even after the invention of the backspring, some *navajas* continued to be constructed without it. Rafael Ocete Rubio mentions them in passing in his text *Armas Blancas en España*, where he informs us that

> although there exist *navajas* lacking backsprings—
> such as the typical Portuguese *navajas* with wooden
> handles, and other crude ones, called "*taponeras*,"
> used in the shops of Jerez de la Frontera—the majority
> have a backspring in the upper part of the handle to
> keep the blade straight when open or maintain it in
> the handles when closed.

While Ocete's main point is that the majority of *navajas* have backsprings, his statement makes it clear that knives from certain regions were constructed without them. Such being the case, and in view of the fact that the introduction of backsprings occurred just about 100 years before the manual's publication, it is not surprising for the author to exhort his preference for *navajas* that had them.

SECOND LESSON
OF THE NAMES BY WHICH
THE *NAVAJA* IS KNOWN

The *navaja* is known by various names among those individuals skilled in its use. We cannot list them all here, but only those that are most frequently used, since every province is accustomed to using its own term.

In Andalusia it is called the *mojosa*, the *chaira*, the *tea*; and in Seville those of great length are known as *las del Santólio*,[4] but in the prisons and jails, and among the *barateros* of Madrid and other places, it is known by such names as *corte*,[5] *herramienta*,[6] *pincho*,[7] *hierro*,[8] *abanico*,[9] *alfiler*,[10] and others. In our lessons, we will refer to it by the generic term of *navaja*.

Translator's comment:

The almost-certain lethality that resulted from the use of large *navajas* earned them the name *santólios*. The term is a contraction of the words *santo*, or "holy," and *olio*, "oil," and typically refers to the unguents that are administered during the Catholic sacrament of Extreme Unction, or last rites to the dying. *Santólio* became popular as slang for large *navajas* because Spaniards of old were convinced that the person having the misfortune of confronting a knife of such proportions would invariably require the administration of last rites.

Curiously, one common name that is glaringly missing from those listed in the manual is *faca*, a term popular in Portugal as well as in Andalusian Spain. This term accompanied the Portuguese during their colonization of Brazil, where it remains in use today. It was from *faca* that the more recent term *facón*, the large knife of the gaucho, derived. In addition to *faca*, many Spanish writers list various other historical and regional terms for the *navaja* in their texts on the subject.

THIRD LESSON
OF POSITIONS OR STANCES

The *diestro* in the handling of the *navaja* has a fundamental position or stance, which, in the same way as with the sword or saber, is known as a guard. After taking the *navaja* in either hand and placing the thumb over the first third of the blade, whose edge should face inward, he should stand on guard at a respectable distance from his opponent, preferably farther than closer, with the free hand resting on the waist in front of the abdomen and ready to receive the *navaja* when he decides to foist it [i.e., change hands].

The feet and legs will be placed equally distant from the opponent, somewhat spread, and in such a way that the body faces frontally, and by no means laterally, as can be seen in the illustration depicted. That is unless one of the hands is holding a hat, cloak, jacket, or shawl, in which case the leg that corresponds to the arm holding the hat or cloak should be placed forward, in the manner depicted by the illustration found in the eighth lesson, "Of Foists."

Upon assuming the guard care must be taken to draw in the abdomen as much as possible, for which effect [the *diestro*] will have to curve inward a bit. [He must do this] without consequently exposing the face too much, for he will be attacked there, and this will be shameful.

The gaze must always remain fixed on that of the opponent in such a manner that it does not waver in any way, even if he attempts to induce this through deceptions, words, or gestures; for we must warn [the reader] that the skillful use of the *navaja* consists essentially of having quickness of eyes and feet, as we shall see further along.

Translator's comment:

The final piece of advice in this lesson is deceptive in its significance. Hispanics from many of Spain's former colonies have inherited a penchant for the use of edged weapons, which in some Sevillian circles is proudly referred to as *el legado andalúz*, or the Andalusian legacy. This legacy is still evident in countries across the globe, from Puerto Rico to the Philippines.

One example of this "legacy" can be found in the Argentine gaucho, still well respected for his deftness with the *facón*, the large sheath knife that accompanies him wherever he goes. The *facón* is the primary weapon used in his indigenous style of knife fighting, known throughout Argentina, Brazil, and Uruguay as *esgrima criolla* (i.e., Creole fencing).

Modern-day exponents of this style, like their Spanish predecessors, also recognize the importance of having quick eyes and feet. In fact, the same attributes highlighted in the present lesson of the manual are still emphasized more than a century later by author José Carlos Depetris in a contemporary essay titled "*El Duelo Criollo*": "The fighting technique—*esgrima criolla*—was based on having a quick eye, whether this were an acquired or innate skill: a quick eye and quicker reflexes, a good reserve of tricks, and a great control of the emotions."

There is little doubt that the origins of this strategy are not only Spanish but also specifically Andalusian for, as Depetris himself affirms,

> The practice of dueling with edged weapons, as a cult of anger or as the only means for addressing an insult, remains embedded since the arrival of the Europeans. The duel appears intimately associated to the first appearance of the gaucho . . . since the time of colonization. Probably its oldest antecedent, one closest to our culture, is the particular combat style of southern Italians and the peninsular Andalusians: a blanket over one arm and a *navaja* in the other.

FOURTH LESSON
METHODS FOR ATTACKING AND DEFENDING ONESELF

After the combatants have assumed their guards, each will be careful not to attack his opponent too suddenly, but rather wait to be attacked in order to properly receive him and discover his level of skill.

For the knowledge of the best way to attack and defend oneself, we will in subsequent lessons explain what is meant by *terreno, jiros* [sic], *contrajiros* [sic], and *cambios*,[11] words whose significance and understanding are indispensable to us.

FIFTH LESSON
OF BOUNDARIES[12]

We refer to as *boundary* that area that can be covered by the full extension of the arm and *navaja*, only within which can an adversary be injured.

Therefore, there will be two boundaries: one your own, the other the opponent's.

SIXTH LESSON
PIVOTS[13] AND HOW TO MAKE THEM

On the *jiros* rests the greatest difficulty of this art: doing them properly requires an admirable speed that can only be acquired through much practice.

With the combatants positioned one in front of the other, leaving in between their boundaries the span of one more boundary, the *diestro* will perform his *jiro* to hurl himself on his opponent and successfully injure him by advancing one of his feet, imperceptibly or suddenly, and turning his body on it [his foot.]

When the fighters are on guard, they cannot reach far enough to injure each other without [first] getting close. The quickest and surest method for accomplishing this is with a *jiro*, which can be repeated two or three times if the one they are aimed at [the opponent] evades them.

The *jiros* can be done on the right side or the left side.

To do them on the right side, and therefore to reach the opponent by his left side, it is necessary to advance with the left foot and turn toward him very quickly. This done, if the opponent does not do a *contrajiro*[14] or a *huida*,[15] he will undoubtedly be injured.

To do them on the left side, pivot on the right foot, at the same time being careful to place the *navaja* in the left hand with which the attack will be delivered, unless, of course, it is already in that hand.

Translator's comment:

The concept of tactical footwork is not unique to Spanish knife use, and most fighting arts, armed and unarmed, recognize its critical importance in personal combat. However, the significance of the *jiro* and *contrajiro* for the *navajero*[16] can be better appreciated when one considers that for him they represented the means to quickly attack (*jiro*) and/or evade (*contrajiro*) when engaging an armed opponent. That is, the *jiro* could be used to "bridge the gap," while the *contrajiro* was used to prevent the opponent from accomplishing the same end. This, in effect, is what the author means when he writes that the *jiro* "can be repeated two or three times." His point is not to suggest that *jiros* are performed consecutively one after another but that, as a tactic, the *jiro* can be used as often as necessary.

SEVENTH LESSON
OF COUNTERPIVOTS[17]

The *contrajiros* are nothing more than the same pivots used by the *diestro* who is attacked with a *jiro*, being careful to do them in the reverse direction from the attacker. That is to say, if attacked with a *jiro* from the right side, turn on the foot of the same side and remove the flank being attacked toward the rear, thus escaping the attack and remaining poised to counterattack the opponent in the rear part of the chest [the back].

The *jiro* is always performed while advancing, the *contrajiro* while retreating. In this manner, an attempted *jiro* is countered

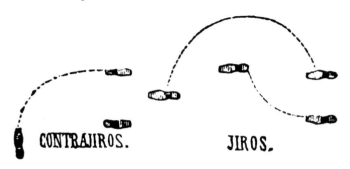

CONTRAJIROS.   JIROS.

by a *contrajiro*, which in turn is countered by a second *jiro*, and so forth. This is the most elegant tactic, and its use reflects skill in the handling of the *navaja*. See the above illustration.

EIGHTH LESSON
FOISTS

Of the various methods there are of fighting with the *navaja*, the best and most reliable is that of using it with both hands; that is to say, being able to use either one for its handling, although there are some who [prefer to] hold their cape, cloak, or hat in their [unarmed] hand. But in addition to there being very little advantage in this mode of fighting, it brings with it many disadvantages that must be taken into consideration.

Certainly, if we note the ease with which we can distract the opponent's vision with a hat held in the hand, and the protection that it provides in the way of a shield against attacks directed to the *diestro*, we should surely adopt this ancient custom of assuming a guard or of fighting with the *navaja*.

Yet, if we stop to examine the many drawbacks and even dangers that go with not being able to foist [the *navaja*] or to attack with anything other than the armed hand, while [noting] at the same time the risk the *diestro* or fighter exposes himself to—as depicted in the illustration—we will undoubtedly realize that the surest and most versatile means [for fighting] is to use both hands for combat. That is, one hand armed and the other unarmed and unencumbered, yet prepositioned to being armed by taking the *navaja* from the [first] hand, which will then be unarmed.

Such is the speed necessary for this tactic, which is called *cambio*,[18] that, given two fighters engaged in combat, the eyesight of one can barely determine in which of the other's hands the *navaja* can be found. In this case, one cannot risk attacking the other unless it is with greater speed, which is another attribute that is equally as necessary as the one explained above.

Our readers should not interpret this to mean that we disapprove of the *diestro* occupying his [unarmed] hand with a hat on all occasions. On the contrary, we condone it in some cases, regarding it more as a special tactic of the art than as a separate style,[19] even though it is regarded as such by some.

To use this tactic during combat, the *diestro* must take care not to take his hat from his head and not to let it fall to the ground in the many moves and evasions that he makes. The objective is to take advantage of it on occasion and hold it in the unarmed hand, or to throw it at the opponent's eyes, or merely feint a throw, as will be explained further along.

In passing, we warn that it is very useful for the *diestro* to wear a sash around his waist, as much to cover part of his belly and somewhat resist *desjarretazos* (ripping slashes) and *viajes* (thrusts to the abdomen) as to execute various tactics with it, which will be described in the proper chapter.

When the *diestro* is challenged or provoked to fight, he must be careful, if he wears a cloak, to discard it in a place where it will not hamper him by getting tangled up with his feet. Under no circumstances will he fight with it on his shoulders, as it will hinder him greatly in his movements, and actually expose him to being injured. We advise the combatants to always shed their cloaks.

The cloak can be quickly removed and in a manner that does not bind the *diestro's* legs. This tactic consists of making a small shrug of the shoulders, while at the same time lightly shaking it loose with the middle part of the arms [i.e., the elbows]. The cloak will end up flat on the ground in the shape of a half moon or fan, in whose center will be standing the fighter.

This method of shedding the cloak without the risk of its wrapping around the *diestro's* feet has as its purpose not losing sight of the opponent, which would certainly be the case if he [the *diestro*] turned his head, as is the tendency to do when throwing the cloak outside of one's boundary. In the latter case he would find himself exposed to being attacked by his opponent before he could even blink.

It should be noted that, unfortunately, not everyone who uses and handles the *navaja* has the generosity and proper intention that one might desire. We give this warning because, as we stated in the Prologue, it is not the fondness that we have toward the art of fighting with the *navaja* or the desire to generalize its teaching that moves us to write this manual. It is merely the [belief] we hold that those ignorant of its handling should become familiar with these rules for when they find themselves attacked by those who abuse it, the same way in which they would abuse any other weapon.

We want to eliminate all concerns, putting on paper and within the reach of all people, the different tactics of the art and the methods—sometimes abhorrent and in poor taste—which are valued by the fighters for assaulting those who do not know how to take the *navaja* in hand. With the reading of this instruction, and with a little bit of practice that can easily be acquired, any pampered young man will be able to defend himself from at least the most sudden attack of any *baratero*.

Translator's comment:

The author's allusion to *escuela aislada* is a clear indication that there existed styles of knife combat different from the one described in his manual. As noted in *Sevillian Steel*, the *baratero* method is merely one of many styles of Spanish knife combat. Throughout Spain there are myriad other styles, generally named after the cities and regions where they developed and continue to be practiced: *catalán*, *manchego*, *toledano*, *vasco*, and so forth.

However, since Spain's explorers and colonizers embarked for the New World from Seville and Cádiz, it was inevitably the Andalusian styles that were brought over from the Old World. References to this style abounded in the literature of the 19th century.

Théophile Gautier, the 19th century French traveler, writer, and martial artist,[20] provides a sober, albeit brief, description of what he and others loosely referred to as the "Andalusian style" in his travelogue *Voyage en Espagne*:

> The *navaja* is the Spaniards' favourite weapon, especially among the lower orders; they wield it with incredible dexterity, making a shield of their cloak, which they roll round the left arm. It is an art which, like fencing, has its own rules, and there are as many masters of knife-play in Andalusia as there are fencing-masters in Paris.

In the classic Romance novel *Carmen*, author Prosper Mérimée describes a brief but colorful account of a fight with *navajas*. The fight scene, narrated by the protagonist, Don José, identifies and contrasts the Andalusian and the Basque styles of knife fighting.

> He drew his knife, and I drew mine. . . . Garcia [Don José's opponent] was already bent double, like a cat ready to spring upon a mouse. He held his hat in his left hand to parry with, and his knife in front of him—that's their Andalusian guard. I stood up in the Navarrese fashion, with my left arm raised, my left leg forward, and my knife held straight along my right thigh.

The author of *Manual del Baratero* further proposes that using a hat in place of a cape or cloak is actually "a special tactic of the art," rather than "a separate style." He makes this deliberate distinction because at the time there were writers like Mérimée who, though otherwise knowledgeable, implied that the hat in the left hand and the *navaja* in the right specifically characterized the Andalusian style.

While these are but two of the many accounts of *navaja* combat described in the French and Spanish literature of the time, it is evident that (1) there was an identifiable Andalusian style and (2) Andalusians did not necessarily share the author's opinion of keeping the off hand empty.

NINTH LESSON
OF ATTACKS

With the two fighters positioned one in front of the other and with *navajas* in hand, each will attempt to injure his opponent, or similarly will begin to work their hands—that is, their *hierros*[21]—with the help of footwork, which is very essential in delivering attacks.

There are many types of attacks that can come from the different positions and tactics used when fighting with the *navaja*. These attacks are known by different names depending on the manner in which they are delivered and the target at which they are aimed, although they all fall under the generic name of *attacks* or *thrusts*.

Before proceeding, we must explain that the body of the *diestro* is composed of two main areas that are referred to as the upper part and the lower part.

By *high line* is meant the half of the body from the waist to the forehead.

By *low line* is meant the half of the body from the waist to the feet. In the same way, attacks will be [designated] high or low, according to whether they strike the high or low lines of the body.

If the *puñalá*,[22] or *mojá*,[23] as the Gypsies call it, is delivered anywhere in the vicinity of the belly, the tactic is known as *atracar*,[24] and the attack is called a *viaje*.[25] Thus, among the *baratero*s it is customary to say, "Let's throw a *viaje*" instead of saying, "Let's fight," or "Let's give a thrust."

When one of the fighters approaches too closely to the other, the latter can very easily injure him by simply extending his arm quickly and thrusting the point of his *navaja* at the high line a few times. Such an attack is known by the term *floretazo*, and no other term is more appropriate for the similarity it shares with the thrust delivered with a foil under similar circumstances, as can be seen in the following illustration. The *floretazo* is not always aimed at the high line, for there is a tactic that is foremost among the safest and most lethal strikes, and which requires the same attack to the center of the low line. The manner in which to deliver this attack will be explained further on.

The *jabeque*, or *chirlo*, is an attack directed to the face, recording on it the sign of disgrace amongst the *barateros*. In effect, of all the injuries that a *diestro* may receive in a fight, none will more accurately demonstrate his poor level of skill, as well as reveal the disregard with which his opponent has treated him.

The act of injuring the face with a thrust is called *enfilar.*[26]

The attack delivered toward the upper part and behind the [target] openings above the ribcages has for its name *desjarretazo.*[27] It is an attack that demonstrates [the *diestro's*] ability to fight, often creating a wide wound in the vertebral column, which is vulgarly called *espinazo*. This is a lethal injury, generally delivered by means of *jiros*.

By *plumada* is understood an attack or slash executed from right to left in a motion describing a curve.

Revés is the name for an attack executed with the hand turned outward from left to right.

The *plumada* and the *revés* are described from the per-spective of the right-handed *diestro*; if done with the left hand, the *plumada* would travel from left to right, and the *revés* from right to left.

TENTH LESSON
PARRIES, EVASIONS

By now our readers should know that the art of fighting with the *navaja* is not based on the mere fancies of some criminal offenders or individuals with wretched lives, but that it is, on the contrary, subject to rules and principles as precise as those of fencing and of the saber. When we come to the discussion of some of the ruses used in the handling of the *navaja*, we will agree with the biggest detractors of this weapon, who believe that the greater core [of the art of the *navaja*] is born of poor breeding and from the most ignoble of sentiments. But until then, and disregarding those actions dis-approved of by wealthy men, whatever class they may hail from, we maintain that the art of fighting with the *navaja* is worthy of being considered in the same light as those of [fighting with] other weapons.

Having already explained the methods of attacking, and the various tactics of those attacks most deserving of our attention, we will now provide an explanation of the parries that are used for defense. This is essential in the handling of every edged weapon, for without it everything pertaining to the means of attacking would be null and without value.

Many believe that the most effective means of fighting with the *navaja* consists of keeping the body constantly in motion, presuming that the *diestro* is ever leaping and racing about. Yet certainly nothing could be further from the truth. The *diestro* fights with calmness and composure, and if he leaps across wide expanses and works with great speed, it is certain that he does so only on given occasions with ample opportunity, more often moving without going beyond a three-foot circle.

His composure allows the *diestro* to be opportunistic in his movements, and this comes only from repeated practice. By such tactics he accustoms his eyes to gauge distances, and thus waits calmly and without fear of his opponent's attack, when he realizes the latter will fall short of reaching him by a half or full inch.

If the attack approaches close within the *diestro's* boundary, he will avoid it by pulling in the threatened target without the need to dodge or leap away. But if the opponent's actions are unknown to the *diestro* because of his speed, or because the attack has entered well into the center of his boundary, he will evade it by leaping backward or to one side far enough not to be reached, and, if possible, to be able himself to reach his attacker. He takes great care not to land on the soles of his feet, but rather on his toes, in order not to be caught unawares, and thus remain ready to leap two, three, four, or more times.

This method of evading is the most common one, but there is another that is more risky albeit secure if done in a timely manner. It consists of the *diestro's* using his unarmed hand to grasp the opponent's weapon arm when the latter approaches to attack.

This type of parry can be done with good form against a *floretazo*, sometimes managing to catch the adversary's wrist. For this reason we warn that such blows [i.e., *floretazos*] must be delivered very quickly, with a willingness to cut the hand or arm [of an opponent who] tries to parry, using for this a quarter of a *plumada* slash.

When a hat is used in fighting, it can be used to parry, trying to disarm the hand of the attacker with a strong blow.

A form of parry that is riskier than all others is frequently used, and it is as follows: when the opponent's weapon arm approaches the *diestro's* boundary by the low line, the latter will escape the attack by throwing a stiff kick at the fingers that hold the *navaja*, which will force [the opponent] to drop it and leave him disarmed. We have said that this is a risky tactic and it is true, for if the *diestro* fails with his intended kick, his opponent will inevitably injure him in a most terrible manner. This

MANUAL OF THE *BARATERO*

could only be prevented by dropping onto the ground while at the same time giving him a kick in the lower abdomen.

ELEVENTH LESSON
RECOURSES

When the rules set forth are not sufficient for the *diestro* to escape his opponent, or to attack him, he will need to resort to his *recourses*—so called because they provide a way out in many instances where skill cannot.

The art of handling the *navaja* has given rise to some recourses that we will only explain briefly, since they primarily belong to the category we call *ruses*, which is covered in the second section of this instruction.

It is necessary to understand that recourses are tactics[28] that enable success where rules do not. From these recourses, every *diestro* practices those that suit him best, or those that he himself has invented.

The deception and feints we will discuss belong to the category of recourses. Here we will describe some recourses.

The *diestro's* hiding of his two hands behind his back so that his adversary cannot see which one holds the *navaja* is a very successful recourse, especially if he first feints with his empty hand prior to using the one that is armed. To accomplish this tactic properly, it is enough to that he lean somewhat toward the feinting side, moving the elbow of that side in the same direction. The opponent will believe he is being attacked from that direction and will naturally dodge, placing his body in the path from which he will receive the actual attack.

Falling to the ground with the naturalness of one who slips, in such a way that the opponent does not suspect deception, is a recourse that, properly executed, ensures the result that the *diestro* seeks. Believing that the *diestro* has accidentally fallen, the opponent will in good faith rush toward him. The *diestro* will raise himself quickly on one knee and receive the opponent with the point of his *navaja*, injuring him in the lower abdomen, as depicted in the preceding

illustration. This is a tactic that requires great speed on the part of the *diestro*.

Similarly, we have witnessed this done while [the *diestro*] simultaneously drops his *navaja* to better deceive the adversary. In the act of getting up, he retrieves the *navaja* from the ground at a significant distance from the opponent. The fall is normally backward. The means of getting up is by bracing one foot and the unarmed hand solidly on the ground and, giving a forceful push with the rest of the body, rising to said position.

NOTES

1. The span of one hand.
2. A skilled individual; one who possesses skill and adroitness in an art or discipline. The exponent when describing the techniques of the *navaja*.
3. Thrusts made with a florete, or fencing foil. Quick thrusts when referring to the *navaja*.
4. Contraction of *santo olio*, or holy oil. A large *navaja*.
5. Edge.
6. Tool.
7. Prick (conventional sense).
8. Iron.
9. Fan.
10. (Sewing) pin.
11. These terms, and the concepts associated with them, are addressed in dedicated chapters that follow.
12. In the manual, *terreno*, which means ground. It is, however, an ambiguous term, and can also mean terrain, real property, or zone. I opted against using ground because there are a number of times the word is used literally to denote floor. I chose to translate it as boundary, since this best captures the author's intended meaning.
13. Properly spelled, *giro*, meaning pivot, turn, or rotation. A pivoting turn used to gain—and to attack from—the opponent's flanks. The noun *giro* derives from the verb *girar*, to pivot, turn, or rotate.
14. A defensive counterturn. See dedicated chapter.
15. Flight. Evasive or retreating movement. See dedicated chapter.
16. Individual skilled in the use of the *navaja*.
17. Properly spelled, *contragiro*, meaning counterpivot. A defensive counterturn or counterrotation. The tactical response to an attempted *giro*.
18. Change (of hands). I chose to translate it as foist, however, because it is the appropriate English term for the tactic of passing the knife from one hand to the other.
19. In the manual, *escuela aislada*, which literally means isolated school. A term referring to any of the individualized styles of knife play practiced throughout Spain. See translator's comments for this lesson.
20. Gautier was well versed in the French fighting systems of savate and la canne. In 1840 he wrote a book titled *The Master of Chausson*. (Chausson was the street form of savate.)
21. Iron or tool. Slang for *navaja*.
22. Contraction for *puñalada*, or knife thrust.
23. Contraction for *mojada*, or wet blow (i.e., a blow that draws blood).
24. To attack. To deliver an aggressive frontal blow to the opponent.
25. Journey or voyage. Slang for a thrust to the belly.
26. To line up or keep straight. Slang for a thrust to the face.
27. Term derived from the verb *desjarretar*, meaning to hamstring or to debilitate. Slang for a ripping slash.
28. In the manual *suple-reglas*, which means semi-rules.

Various Tactics Performed When Fighting with the *Navaja*

FIRST LESSON
GUARD POSITIONS

Our readers have already seen in the first section of this instruction—to the extent possible in a small manual such as this—the principal methods of attack and defense that are used in the practice of the *navaja*. We emphasize principal methods because we can be certain that there as many methods as there are fighters and *baratero*s, and

Los Barateros, by José Luís Pellicer.

it would require a detailed and intensive effort to provide a complete explanation of each one.

Thus, understanding the attacks and parries that are essential to our purpose, we will now move on to explain the way to put them into practice once the fighters are face-to-face and prepared to fight. That is to say that we will show how the *diestro* should proceed according to the different guards he may assume and what benefit he might derive from the understanding he has gained.

In this way it is observable how much a quickness of eye helps in all types of tactics, so much so that the *diestro* in guard position can approach the opponent until reaching his boundary, in spite of the considerable risk of being injured, as long as he is committed to not allow the latter to move his weapon-bearing arm. The slightest move that he makes could get him wounded in the same arm, thus preventing him from attacking. This is a very dangerous tactic because for the two combatants there is only one boundary in which they can wound one another without any movement of the feet and merely extending the arm holding the *navaja*.

The *diestro* can assume the guard position using any of these tactics, but [it must be] with the express condition of never forgetting the position he finds himself in, and of knowing which parts of his body are exposed to the reach of the opponent's *navaja*.

Sometimes we have seen the *diestro* throw himself to the ground, using this tactic as his guard position; this is in fact one of the safest and one in which he has the least possibility of being attacked without imminent risk to the opponent. The only easy means of engaging one who presents himself in this guard position is by receiving his attacks with the hat in your hand.

Whenever the *diestro* attacks his adversary he must do so by either the high line or the low line, as we have said elsewhere. From this it follows that when he delivers an attack, he risks receiving another on the line opposite to the one he has attacked; that is to say, if he aims toward the high line, he leaves the low line open, and if he attacks the low line, he leaves the high line exposed.

It can be said as a general rule that the opportune moment when the *diestro* should wound his opponent is when, after the latter has delivered his attack, he retracts his weapon arm, which was unable to "find flesh," to borrow an expression from the *barateros*. It is necessary to remain calm, and watch carefully for that moment that should be seized without delay. And if he does not succeed in his objective, he must retreat as quickly and as low as possible to avoid being attacked in turn when retracting the arm.

Translator's comment:

Here again the author alludes to the variety of methods that were practiced in the handling of the *navaja*. He goes so far as to state that there could be as many methods of *tirar la navaja*[1] as there were *tiradores*.[2]

The statement is corroborated by Gautier who, in *Voyage en Espagne*, comments on the variety of *navaja* combat styles he witnessed during his travels:

Everyone who uses the knife has his own secret thrusts and special ways of stabbing; they say that adepts of the art can recognize the artist responsible for a wound from the look of it, just as we recognize a painter by his touch.

SECOND LESSON
ATTACKS FROM THE FRONT

We will now explain the thrusts that are appropriate for various tactics executed while crossing boundaries. It may seem strange to many of our readers that we have not spoken of these while discussing the various types of attacks that we described in the first section of this Instruction. But to such readers we say that we prefer to explain in this second section *attacks from the front* and *from the flanks* separately from the rest. After discussing *guard positions* in the previous lesson, we believe we should address, in this and the following one, attacks that are initiated from the movements already learned.

By *attacks from the front* we mean those that the combatants initiate while face-to-face, without trying to attack the flanks or resorting to ruses. With the *diestro* in guard position, he begins approaching his opponent until he crosses the boundaries; then, raising his armed hand quickly, he delivers a *plumada* that will injure the latter if he fails to evade or parry it, which can be accomplished by extending his arm at the same time to deliver a *floretazo*.

Translator's comment:
An example of the frontal attacks discussed in this lesson is presented in *The Secret History of the Sword*, where J. Christoph Amberger describes an account of a *navaja* duel documented in the German text *Duelbuch*, published in 1869. An excerpt from the full account in Amberger's book reads as follows:

The witnesses of the duel had barely noted this when the injured man jumped with a powerful lunge at his opponent, ran under him, and with his wide knife delivered a thrust into his lower body that the other one had no time to parry. With a muted scream he reached for the wound, swayed, and fell to the ground. With one cut, the knife had opened up the body in a foot-long incision, so the entrails came out.

THIRD LESSON
ATTACKS FROM THE FLANK

Attacks from the flank are those that the combatants initiate when seeking unprotected targets and rib cages; they are delivered during *jiros* and *contrajiros*, and often during passes.

FOURTH LESSON
CORRIDAS

The *corrida*[3] is one of the most common tactics used among fighters; and we can be certain, without fear of contradiction, that it is the most essential tactic of this art because it encompasses all of the ways of attacking the opponent or, as is said among *barateros*, of *finding his bulk*. The opponent will have to defend himself or flee. From the *corridas*, every kind of attack can be initiated, or, better said, the *corridas* represent the entire art.

The *corrida* is nothing more than the describing of a semicircle on the ground by each one of the combatants in the act of fighting. They must always be careful to maintain a basic distance between themselves until the moment to attack is at hand, in which case there will be a need to enter the opponent's boundary and injure him with any of the attacks learned.

The *corrida* is accomplished by moving to one side arbitrarily without altering the initial guard position, sometimes toward the left, other times toward the right. Whenever one of the fighters attacks the other, the latter performs a *jiro* or dodges with a *corrida* in the opposite direction. Or he can give up his ground by leaping away. The result of this is that the two semicircles formed by the combatants, one in front of the other, ultimately describe one complete circle, more or less perfect, and of varying visibility. Whatever speed the *diestro* possesses in his feet, so much the better will he perform his *corrida* because, as we have already said, this art is more based on the agility and cold-bloodedness of the *diestro* than on anything else. So while technique is essential, it is useless without the help of these two qualities.

Translator's comment:

It is evident that the strategy of the *corrida* described in this lesson was influenced by, if not directly related to, the Spanish Circle theory of fencing. A practical understanding of the Spanish Circle was at the crux of the art of *Destreza*. Absent this understanding, the Spanish swordsman was little different from the swordsmen of the other styles. Mastery of the Spanish Circle, on the other hand, set the Spaniard apart from, and arguably above, his French and Italian contemporaries.

Although the comprehensiveness of the *Destreza* style prohibits a proper explanation of it here, at its core was the concept of responding to the opponent's approaches and overtures by circling him without increasing or decreasing the distance from him. The Spaniard's stepping patterns were geometrical in direction and precise in execution.

Ultimately, when the opponent's impatience or overconfidence induced him to miscalculate his attack, the *diestro* versed in the Spanish Circle would capitalize on the error and allow his adversary to impale himself by his own precipitous action. "Who controls the distance controls the fight," is an old adage common to both sword and knife fighting.

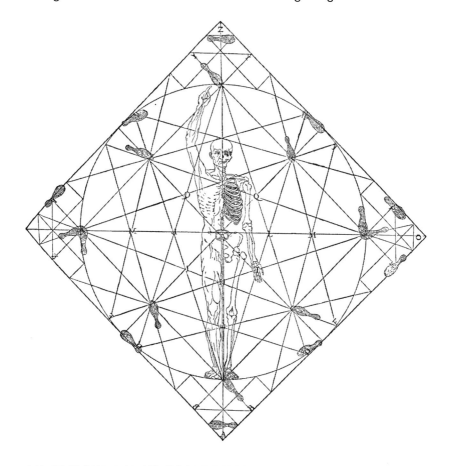

FIFTH LESSON
MOLINETE

When the opponent approaches too close to the *diestro*, the latter should respond with the *molinete*,[4] which consists of lifting one of his feet off the ground and turning around on the other with great speed, then stopping suddenly to extend his arm and deliver a *floretazo* to the attacker.

Bear in mind that this tactic is very dangerous and that the best time to use it is when the adversary attempts an attack toward your low line, but it should never be used when the attack is to the high line. As we have already indicated, the *floretazo* is almost always aimed at the high line, and its use requires that the opponent be threatening the low line.

If the *diestro* finds himself too constrained in the high line, that is, if he is attacked by the opponent from deep within his own boundary, he will respond by lowering his body until the knee touches the ground, then introducing the *navaja* toward the [opponent's] lower abdomen. See the illustration for the eleventh lesson, first section.

We must note here that, as much with the *molinete* as with the high *floretazos*, the *diestro* risks having his weapon arm grabbed by the adversary's free hand and having his wrist turned back toward his own throat, thus injuring himself with his own *navaja*.

Translator's comment:
The technique that the author identifies as the *molinete*, i.e. "lifting one of his feet off the ground and turning around

on the other with great speed, then stopping," is also known, albeit vulgarly, as the *cuadrada*.

As described in *Sevillian Steel*, the *cuadrada* is initiated from the standard combat crouch position. As the attacker executes and commits himself to his thrust, you bring your rear left leg sweeping around *behind* your lead right leg. As you do this, you simultaneously thrust the *navaja* forward.

This counterthrust should be aimed high, and your primary target should be the throat. Alternative targets can be the midsection or right rib cage. Again, use the ball of your right foot as a pivot point. Recover quickly from your counter and reorient yourself to his position.

The other technique described in this lesson, "lowering his body until the knee touches the ground, then introducing the *navaja* toward the [opponent's] lower abdomen," is also known as the *pasada baja.*

Actually, the knee should *not* touch the ground because under adrenalized combat conditions the impact can easily damage the knee, cause a predictable degree of pain, and divert one's attention from the threat at hand.

The *pasada baja*, as described in *Sevillian Steel*, is also initiated from the combat crouch. As the attacker commits to his thrust, your right leg slides forward and your left knee drops almost to a kneeling position. Do not, however, allow the knee to hit the ground. As you drop, bring the left hand to the ground to brace yourself, and thrust the *navaja* forward.

When executing this tactic, lower your head as you brace, and resist the impulse to look at the attacker's knife. This counterthrust is aimed high, and your target should be the abdomen or groin. Alternative targets can be the right thigh or stomach. Once again, recover quickly and reorient yourself to his position.

Both the *cuadrada* and the *pasada baja* are Spanish versions of Italian sword techniques that were co-opted for use with the *navaja*. The Spanish names for these techniques are corruptions of the Italian terms *in quartata* and *pasatta sotto*, respectively.

SIXTH LESSON
THROWING THE *NAVAJA*

Among many fighters, and more commonly among sailors, it is customary to throw the *navaja* at the opponent's body. [The *navaja*] is carried tethered to the waist by means of a long cord or a chain made of thin wire.

It will seem incredible to some of our readers the enormous accuracy we have witnessed in the throwing of the *navaja*, leaving it stuck in the chest or the abdomen, precisely in the spot that the *diestro* had intended, but there is nothing more certain. And such admirable ability is comparable only to that demonstrated by the intended victim, who can often avoid the attack, and even seize the connecting cord and cut it with his own [*navaja*].

While we greatly admire such agility and skill, we advise fighters never to use this tactic because of how uncertain and dangerous it is—this despite the fact that there are men who can do this with great precision, which can only be attributed to the continual practice they have undertaken since boyhood.

SEVENTH LESSON
MOVEMENTS WITH THE HAND AND HAT

Since we have already seen that steadiness and quickness of eye is what most contributes to the handling of the *navaja*, we will explain the means that fighters use to force the opponent to shift his gaze or close his eyes. After the *diestro* has feinted or delivered some strikes and wants to distract the adversary's sight to attack him, he should at the same time [that] he attacks pass his unarmed hand in front of the other's eyes. Or, taking the hat that he's wearing, he should pass it one or more times in the same manner, in which instant he should attack the other's low line, injuring him in the abdomen.

Translator's comment:
The great importance that Spaniards place on eyesight and

vision in edged-weapons combat is again emphasized in this lesson. Spanish knife fighters, like swordsmen, train not only to deprive their opponent of eyesight but also to resist being deprived of their own. Like all other tried-and-true methods, this attribute has been bequeathed to us from the past.

In an English-language journal that came out some 25 years after the publication of *Manual del Baratero*, an article describes the writer's encounter with "a young man who seemed likely to know how to use the knife." Following is an excerpt from that article from the *Appletons' Journal*:

> The national weapon of the Spaniards is the knife, and certainly they know how to use it. Talking one day with a young man who seemed likely to know, I asked him what there was peculiar in the management of the knife.
>
> "Why," said he, with a smile, "I could kill you, and you couldn't kill me."
>
> "Well," said I, "please point out the difference between us. What would you do first?"
>
> "Why, I'd make you wink, and stab you while you winked!"
>
> "How would you make me wink?"
>
> "Why, so," said he, throwing up his left hand near my eyes.
>
> "Well, I could do the same."
>
> "Try it," said he.
>
> I tried, and found it impossible to make him blink, though I passed my hand up and down several times so as almost to touch his eyelashes.
>
> His bright, black eyes looked out at me unflinchingly all the while. It was clear that his eyes were educated, and that mine were not.

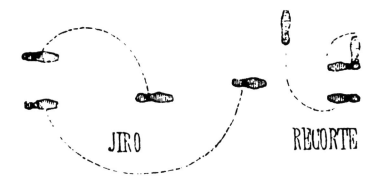

JIRO   RECORTE

EIGHTH LESSON
RECORTES

The *recorte* is nothing more than a *jiro*, with the difference that when initiating it the *diestro* turns his back toward the opponent. The *jiro*, on the other hand, must always be executed while facing the opponent.

[The *recorte*] is appropriate when the *diestro* is attacked with a *jiro* toward his vertebral column and is very dangerous.[5]

NINTH LESSON
TACTIC OF THE SNAKE

The tactic of the snake consists of the *diestro* throwing himself on the ground. While supporting himself with his unarmed hand, he advances toward the opponent's boundary to injure him in his lower abdomen with either a *floretazo* or a *plumada*.

Translator's comment:
The author's reference to using the *floretazo* may be confusing to some, after reading in Lesson Five that "the *floretazo* is almost always aimed at the high line." Actually, there is not really a contradiction here. When used *offensively*, that is, in initiating an attack, the *floretazo is* generally aimed at the face,

MANUAL OF THE *BARATERO*

chest, or midsection. However, when used *defensively*, it usually means that the opponent is attacking the high line himself, leaving only his low line open to counter. In such cases, the *floretazo* is aimed to the abdomen, groin, or lead thigh.

That said, however, it should be noted that the *suerte* described in this lesson is unheard of in the contemporary *navaja* arts. The *diestro* attempting this tactic would have to be extremely confident of his skills, since throwing himself on the ground would severely restrict his mobility, as well as his subsequent ability to evade the opponent's potential counterattack.

TENTH LESSON
DECEPTIONS

Every attack can be true or feigned.

We call it true when the intention of the *diestro* is to injure his adversary.

It is considered feigned when the *diestro* uses it only with an end toward deceiving and catching his opponent unawares.

Therefore, in thrusts delivered from the front, the attack is feigned toward the low line in order to actually attack the high line, and vice versa.

If the *diestro* is threatened on the high line, he will naturally move to defend there with his *navaja* if he does not understand feints, only to end up exposing his low line to the true attack. If threatened on the low line, he will cover there with his armed hand, while the true attack goes to the high line, generally a thrust to the face.

It can be established, as a general rule, that every true attack can be made into a feigned attack; that is, a deception, and every feigned attack can be made into a true attack.

Feints can be equally accomplished with *jiros* and *contrajiros*, and in this manner the *diestro,* for example, will feint toward one side. In so doing, he will deceive his opponent into doing the corresponding *contrajiro*, thereby exposing an opening for the true attack.

ELEVENTH LESSON
RUSES[6]

We now come to a subject in which we understandably side with those individuals who abhor the art of handling the *navaja*. To be sure, if we did not focus on anything else but on the results of some of the ruses that are used by certain fighters, we would proclaim the art as immoral and highly ignoble. But our readers have already seen the fundamental rules we have laid out in the course of this instruction and will recognize that not everything in the art of fighting with the *navaja* is vile and reproachable. On the contrary, it should be regarded as subject to the same general principles as is the art of any other weapon.

We would not want the various ruses employed by base and cowardly men to result in a mistaken impression with regard to fighters who use *navajas*. The abuses done with the weapon are not a part of this art. Those who use the *navaja* in such manner would act the same way if they used a sword or a saber.

We would prefer to refrain from presenting [these ruses] due to how repugnant they appear to us, and how distant they are from the objectives that led to the writing of this manual. At the same time, however, it is not possible to avoid speaking of some ruses that we believe are adaptable in extreme cases, or which would enable the unjustly attacked individual to avoid [such an attack].

We have already stated in the first section that some ruses can be performed with the sash that the *diestro* wears round his waist, and such is true. In the various maneuvering that takes place while fighting, when the *diestro* decides to apply a ruse with the sash, he needs only to untie one end and let it drag along the ground. In this way his opponent will easily step on it, in which case quickly pulling it will cause [his opponent] to fall to the ground or trip badly.

There is another ruse with the sash, and it is as follows: placing coins, rocks, or anything else of significant weight on one end of it, the *diestro* hurls it violently around his adversary's legs, who will then find himself entangled and unable to move, and thus exposed to being injured.

The hat can be thrown at the opponent's face, and this is regarded as an effective ruse.

Sometimes the *diestro* picks up a fistful of dirt, if this is available where the fighting takes place, throws it in the eyes of his adversary, and moves in to attack without delay.

The *diestro* can also step on one of his opponent's feet with his own, and this can result in a successful ruse if the latter fails to escape it.

The *diestro* can also give his opponent a strong kick in the abdomen, or trip the [opponent's] legs with his own, causing him to fall to the ground.

The *diestro* can look behind the opponent, who will be led to believe that there is someone at his back and, turning his head, fall victim to the [*diestro's*] attack.

"Stop, you're going to trip," says the *diestro* to his opponent, with the object of making him look at the ground, and in doing so [the *diestro*] injures him.

Finally, so many are the ruses used by fighters that it would require much time to explain them all. Thus, we are content in listing the most common and general ones.

Translator's comments:

The so-called ruse of causing an opponent to trip or become ensnared in some item of apparel is as prevalent in knife literature as it is absurd. This ruse has been similarly touted in descriptions of Gypsy, Mexican, and Argentinean knife combat. There even exist descriptions of this ruse during "documented" knife-fights in the Old West. An entry in *The Cowboy Encyclopedia* presents a classic example. Here, the eloquent (if politically incorrect) author, Bruce Grant, informs us that "knife fighters tried all kinds of tricks to throw each other off guard. Sometimes a knife fighter would back up, trailing his poncho on the ground. If the other stepped on it he jerked it and threw his opponent off balance."

As stated earlier in this translation, many of the techniques found in the manual are comedic in their strategic naiveté. One can only conclude that through repeated, *albeit undocumented*, accounts of its occurrence, this "ruse" has taken on the role of a knife-fighting urban legend. Thus, unless one is defending against a blind attacker, the ruse of the trailing sash, cloak, or poncho deserves to be relegated to its rightful place, alongside albino alligators and other urban legends, in the toilet.

NOTES

1. Knife play.
2. Fighters.
3. *Corrida* means a run or chase. In the manual, it refers to the footwork used by opponents to circle and maneuver against one another during a knife fight.
4. Small windmill.
5. In the manual, *espuesto*; this is a misspelling of *expuesto*, which can mean exposed or, more appropriately, dangerous.
6. The Spanish name for this lesson, *tretas*, means feints of the type used in fencing. Its use in the manual, however, makes it clear that the term is intended to denote ruses.

The Proper Way to Handle the *Cuchillo*

Fencing with the Puñal, by Gustave Doré.

FIRST LESSON
OF THE *CUCHILLO*[1]

There is little we can say of the *cuchillo* and *puñal*, their handling being to a great extent subject to the rules we have given for fighting with the *navaja*. We need only note that attacks with the knife are always delivered with the point, and that these have no other name than thrusts.

Sailors frequently use the *cuchillo*, and, in the jails and prisons, it is with this weapon that killers frequently "exact their commissions."[2]

Translator's comment:

In *Spain*, Davillier corroborates the author's information with regard to the thrusting use of the fixed-blade knife and proceeds to describe the weapon as follows:

> Like the *navaja*, the *puñal* has its own particular rules. This weapon finds patrons among sailors and prisoners, and is distinguished from the former by its being used only for thrusts. The handle is short and thick, and has something of an egg shape; as to the blade, it is sometimes flat and oval, sometimes round, and sometimes four-sided.

SECOND LESSON
STANCES

The safest stance for using the *cuchillo* or *puñal* is the one depicted by the illustration below. The *cuchillo* is held in the right hand in the manner most comfortable for the *diestro*. The cloak, jacket, or shawl is draped over the left arm, or a fishing net or thick piece of leather can be used, as the *baratero*s do, to stop thrusts and obstruct the opponent's vision. The stance is not the same as is used in fighting with the *navaja*, for in handling the *cuchillo* the *diestro* positions himself with the left arm and leg toward the opponent.

Lacking anything else to protect the weaponless arm, it is common to hold a hat or cap in the hand. In all other ways it [handling the *cuchillo*] is the same as has been said with regard to the *navaja*.

THIRD LESSON
ATTACKS; METHODS OF THROWING THE *PUÑAL*

The attacks with the *cuchillo* and *puñal* are always delivered with one hand; that is to say, foists are not used. By the same token, attacks are always aimed at the opponent's unarmed side, being careful to injure him on the left flank, [a] more reliable [method].

The *jiros* are also used to good effect, although only the ones to the right side are valuable, as are similarly the *contrjiros* to the left.

The *cuchillo*[3] is thrown at the opponent's body by extending it over the palm of the hand with the handle facing outward. Thus held, it is thrown forcefully and sticks, unless the opponent moves his body by leaping or hitting the ground.

FOURTH LESSON
EVASIONS AND ESCAPES

The evasions and escapes are exactly the same as in the handling of the *navaja*; refer to what is explained in that section.

FIFTH LESSON
RECOURSES AND RUSES[4]

See what we have written regarding recources and ruses for the *navaja*.

SIXTH LESSON
DEFENSES AGAINST THE *PUÑAL*

If on some occasion the *diestro* should find himself without a *cuchillo*, as tends to happen, and if he is confronted by one of the many bad-intentioned men with either a *cuchillo* or *puñal* in hand, he does not under such circumstances have to run. He would be wrong to do so. What he should do is wait in guard position with his hat in the right[5] hand or, without it, with his arm raised so that the hand is held higher than his head, exposing all of his chest, as depicted in the following illustration.

When the opponent initiates his thrust, the *diestro* will defend himself by striking a blow to the [opponent's] wrist with his hand. If possible, he should grab it from underneath; if not, he should not panic but step backward with his left leg, pulling in his body, and raising his right arm to position it behind the opponent's left arm. Grasping the center of the left arm, he will throw his left hand behind the opponent's neck, being certain to make all movements without fear, and quickly he will succeed in defending himself.

And if the opponent who finds himself in this position when his intended action fails decides to turn to repeat his attack, the *diestro* will at the same time help him up [while] pushing him so that his own weapon does him harm.

Translator's comments:

In 1805, a Spaniard named Manuel Antonio de Brea published a fencing treatise titled *Principios de Destreza del Espadín*, or *Fencing Principles of the Smallsword*. Although the greater part of the treatise concerns itself with the subtleties and complexities of swordsmanship, its twenty-second chapter is dedicated to instructing the reader on how to engage a knife-bearing attacker when one happens to be unarmed. That chapter is titled *Defensa Contra el Puñal*. After reading the technique described in *Manual del Baratero,* it becomes evident that its author lifted the present lesson verbatim from *Destreza del Espadín.*

When I first read this lesson in *Manual del Baratero,* I was confused by the author's incomprehensible explanation of the knife defense. It was not until years later, when I acquired a copy of *Destreza del Espadín,* that the technique in *Baratero* ultimately made sense.

The confusion inherent in the *Manual del Baratero*'s description arises from the fact that its author, Mariano de Rementeria y Fica, inexplicably substituted the words "left" for "right" and vice versa when he plagiarized the lesson. Adding to this confusion is the fact that, at one point, the *Manual del Baratero*'s text describes the diestro with his "[right] arm raised with the hand held higher than his head," while the accompanying illustration depicts him with his left arm raised. Fortunately, when read as it was originally written in *Destreza,* the mechanics of the technique finally become intelligible:

> When the opponent initiates his thrust, the diestro will defend himself by striking a blow to the [opponent's] wrist with his hand. If possible, he should grab it from underneath; if not, he should not panic but step backward with his [right] leg, pulling in his body, and raising his [left] arm to position it behind the opponent's [right] arm. Grasping the center of the [right] arm, he will throw his left hand behind the opponent's neck, being certain to make all movements without fear, and quickly, he will succeed in defending himself.

NOTES

1. Fixed-blade knife. The author, however, addresses both the *cuchillo* and the *puñal,* or thrusting dagger, indiscriminately in this section of the manual.
2. In the manual, *cobrar el barato.*
3. The author indicates *cuchillo,* while the title of this lesson states *puñal.*
4. Feints of the type used in fencing. Its use in the manual, however, makes it clear that the term is used to denote *ruses.*
5. Note: The corresponding illustration depicts the *diestro* with his *left* arm raised.

The Way the Gypsies Handle the Scissors

FIRST LESSON
OF THE SCISSORS

The Gypsies are the only ones who handle this type of weapon, no doubt because they are generally dedicated to the selling and grooming of horses. They carry [scissors] to trim mules and ponies. There are also Aragonese grooms.

Duel with the Santólios, by Gustave Doré.

We will excuse ourselves from describing their mechanism, since none of our readers lacks this knowledge.

Translator's comments:

The weapons the author refers to as *tijeras*, or scissors, were actually the mule shears used by horse grooms to trim the manes of horses and mules. Such shears are properly called *cachas*, and not *tijeras*, which refers specifically to scissors of the type used by barbers and tailors. Horse grooming was almost exclusively a *Gitano* trade, and one that they were renown for throughout all of Spain. The *cachas* were recognized and accepted as a tool of their trade.

Although it requires no great stretch of the imagination to intuitively use scissors or shears as a weapon, scant written records survives on the specific techniques. What little more information exists again comes from the travel writers of that time, and both Charles Davillier and George Borrow remark on the scissors' use in combat in their writings about *Gitanos*. Davillier indicates that the *cachas* offered an alternative to the *navaja* as a weapon of combat: "Sometimes it is the formidable *navaja*, its blade long and sharp, that is their weapon of combat, but the *cachas*—long scissors that they use to clip and groom their beasts of burden—are very terrible as well."

Borrow, the English missionary who brought the Bible to the Romany and lived among them for many years, also provides some background on their use. In *Zincali: An Account of the Gypsies in Spain*, he reveals that

in the girdle of the *esquilador*[1] are stuck the large scissors called in Spanish *tijeras*, and in the Gypsy tongue *cachas*, with which he principally works . . . . The *Gitanos* are in general very expert in the use of the *cachas*, which they handle in a manner practised nowhere but in Spain; and with this instrument the poorer class principally obtain their bread.

The reader partial to the Romany peoples is cautioned that *Zincali* was written over 100 years ago. Borrow was living in a time and place that was not sympathetic toward Gypsies. Yet, while his tone may sound racist today, Borrow's writing is relatively objective for his time; his actual efforts in writing *Zincali* are probably a result of his spending many years among the *Gitanos*.

SECOND LESSON
METHODS OF HANDLING THEM

The methods of handling the scissors in fighting are the same as we have already explained for the *cuchillo*. We have only to add that, held open by the center formed by its four limbs, the wound [that the scissors] produce is normally with the two points, and always lethal.

We have nothing more to say on the handling of this weapon that has not already been said of the *navaja* and the *cuchillo,* having [the scissors] in their place, and the rules being the same for the three weapons.[2]

Translator's comments:

According to Davillier and Borrow, the *cachas* were carried in a leather sheath and worn at the waist like a sailor's knife. As such, the shears were ever present in an innocuous manner. Davillier observes that "they almost always carry them suspended from their waists in a case that contains shears of different sizes; in the event of a duel, it is not long before they are used to put up their guards."

The most common way to hold *cachas* and scissors is like a knife, in a forward grip, with the ring and little fingers inserted through the scissors' bottom-most finger hole. This enables one to deliver hard thrusts without the hand's losing its grip on impact. It allows the scissors to be used in a variety of *puñalada*-type thrusts. Additionally, the forward grip affords the greatest reach with the scissors, a benefit necessary if the opponent is armed with a *navaja* or some other form of edged weapon.

Although he contradicts the fact that the *cachas* were held and used closed, like a knife, Davillier's narrative makes it clear that they were formidable weapons themselves, not only because of the *Gitanos'* skill in handling them, but also because of their prodigious dimensions:

> The lengths of these large scissors reach almost a foot-and-a-half; only instead of having them closed and using them like a *puñal* or *navaja*, they keep them opened, tightly held in their dark and calloused hands at the point where the two blades intersect.

In Part II, Chapter I of *Zincali,* Borrow quotes a Gypsy who boasts of his ability to wield the shears against Spaniards:

> "We are much looked after by the Busne,[3] who hold us in great dread, and abhor us. Sometimes, when wandering about, we are attacked by the labourers, and then we defend ourselves as well as we can. There is no better weapon in the hands of a *Gitano* than his *cachas* or shears, with which he trims the mules. I once snipped off the nose of a Busne, and opened the greater part of his cheek in an affray up the country near Trujillo."

In essence, due to their design, shears and scissors lend themselves to tactical applications not possible with a knife. When used in conjunction with a knife, they become an effective defensive tool, capably intercepting an opponent's attack while enabling the *navajero* to simultaneously deliver his own. Their two-bladed design also doubles their potential lethality as a projectile weapon.

END NOTES

1. Horse groom.
2. In the arts of *acero sevillano* there are various other methods of using shears and scissors as weapons. Whether these methods were developed subsequent to the writing of *Manual del Baratero* or whether its author was simply unaware of them remains a matter of conjecture.
3. "Spaniard" in caló, the dialect of Spanish Gypsies.

The *Baratero*

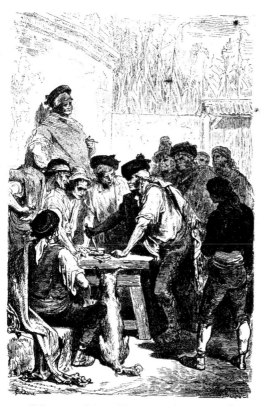

El Baratero Cobra el Barato, by Gustave Doré.

In Spain there exist particularly unique individuals the likes of which cannot be found in other countries. None, however, is as remarkable as the *baratero*; that is, the killer who forcefully exacts a commission within the gamblers' circles known as *garitos*. This renegade individual, normally hailing from the dregs of society and raised in jails and prisons, frequently comes to a tragic end brought about by his own misdeeds, either on a beach or [in] a field, or at the hands of another who is tougher or luckier than he. Another who rips open his guts before an audience made up of lowlifes, soldiers, thieves, and Gypsies. It befalls him, in the center of a small town square or clearing, upon a platform of significant height, at the hands of the law's executioner who, after asking the usual "Do you forgive me," squeezes and rearranges his throat[1] with the greatest indifference, as he places a Biscayan bowtie[2] around it.

There are three known types of *barateros*: the troop *baratero*, the prison *baratero*, and the beach *baratero*. We will speak of each in turn.

The troop *baratero*, educated in the barracks and mess halls where he underwent his difficult apprenticeship, can be recognized by his bullying and life-sparing airs, his dandy-like posturing, and the ever-present cigarette or cigar in his mouth, while another is tucked behind his ear.

His hair is the longest of all the soldiers in his company, his hat is tilted to one side, and his tunic unbuttoned at the chest, its collar turned outward. One hand is thrust in his pants pocket, and on the other, resting on his hip, can be seen a small tin ring on his little finger. He spits through his teeth, speaks in Andalusian and caló,[3] is very dark skinned, invariably ugly, and even more so if he is cross-eyed. He wears his mustache sometimes short and sometimes upturned, Burgundian style. He speaks while blinking his eye and bouncing his foot.

He is the company[4] loudmouth, [but] the first sergeant excuses him from barracks duties because he sometimes needs money and [the *baratero*] lends it to him from his own pocket. His pockets overflow, thanks to the stabbings and scams in which he is so well versed, and this has earned him high regard and great influence among his comrades.

The company *baratero* is the laziest man in it; he knows little of [military] exercises and completely despises taking orders. On the other hand, he handles the tool of his trade like no other and is an expert at playing *chapas*, *brisca*, *cané*, and *treinta y una*.[5] He gets drunk, has a woman—who is the barracks waitress—and makes everyone obey him. During military campaigns he carries himself as a leader because he is brave and is the first to pillage, since he has sticky fingers.[6]

He searches out the gambling dens in the towns that he frequents, and there he plays out his routines among the most forsaken individuals with whom he associates, and who often repay his kindness and sympathy with a beating or a couple of knife thrusts, which he has earned for some form of dirty card dealing.

This *baratero* is the born enemy of his countrymen, whom he calls masters.[7] At the drop of a hat he will confront the first person who crosses his path and whom he believes has given him a dirty look, and ends up causing a rumpus like the devil himself. When his colonel hears of the scandal and sends him to the stockade, he is released two days later, huffing and puffing, and anxious to start up again with anyone. He gives his sweetheart a daily beating and abandons her for [another's girl], who follows him, and whom he will also abandon at the first infidelity.

When his regiment stays overnight in another town, the *baratero* is visited by every other *baratero* in the vicinity. These are often deserters, hiding from the hounds of justice. They refer to themselves as *comrades*, go drinking together, and raise a few glasses, which they may eventually toss in each other's faces at the slightest contradiction or gesture. They will step out onto the street and, clutching their *navajas*, let loose two or three slashes, which will serve to sow deep roots in their friendship. Together they will visit the gambling dens that they operate, on the expressed condition of not disturbing anyone or horning in on each other's rackets.

Let us continue with the *baratero* of the prisons. This one is of the type most feared by all. Since boyhood he has been a killer, a vocation in which he learned the many ways of disemboweling. During his free hours, which were many, he entertained himself by picking the pockets of his well-to-do neighbors, or by anything that brought him luck.

He could, at first sight, recognize the yokel or bumpkin. He would cheat them at the slightest pretext and separate them without warning from their money, which he would then use to play *cané* with the other guys, whose belongings he would "win" through either trickery or obscene threats.

If, in spite of everything, he was the type to who easily forgot himself due to his temperament and sticky fingers, he would draw his *navaja* and force everyone to hand over their winnings. This made him appear manly among the young rascals and gangs of the city. It was thus that he grew old in years and in villainy, leaving his well-established mark in the taverns, jails, and gambling dens where he enjoyed a great distinction.

In the end, his reputation well established, and having made himself feared among all the toughs of the slaughterhouse, his misdeeds and foul mouth brought him to jail for the twentieth time. Once there, he was not satisfied by his great status among the prisoners but instead strove for more and got it.

About twenty of them were playing *chapas* in the prison courtyard when our man reaches their group, coughs in his particular manner and—eyeing a *navaja* thrust deeply into the floor—asks in a hoarse but calm voice:

"Whose is that trifling knife?"

"Mine," responds its owner with a horrifying gesture, "and no one eats here but me."

"Well, comrade, [the knife's presence] upsets my stomach and I want to throw up." Kicking it with his foot, he causes [the *navaja*] to roll a good stretch along the floor.

You should have heard the fuss, poor souls! The one who collected the money bravely defended his well-earned right, but not so well that our Chato[8] (we must call him *something*) can't thrust his *navaja* into [the other's] abdomen. You could cut the air with great admiration [coming from] the honored bystanders. Since that time, he is the *baratero* of the jail and no one coughs at him, [as he] fulfills his duties without having his dignity challenged.

Would you, curious readers, want to meet our good Chato among that crowd stirring up a furor in the courtyard? Look toward the right, among that group of felons, and you have met him. He is shorter than he is tall, broad of shoulders, [with] a repugnant and stupid-looking face, big sideburns, long curls over his forehead pulled to one side, and a somewhat drooping left eyebrow.

His attire is in proper proportion to his figure: wide pants of green corduroy, held at the waist by an ill-fitting woolen sash. The latter at the same time serves as his purse, where he keeps his money, his *navaja,* and his deck of cards. For shoes, he wears either rope-soled sandals or cowhide half-boots, which are quite grotesque. He is generally in shirt-sleeves and wears a green handkerchief tied around his head, giving him a sinister and horrifying look.

Forgive us for saying that his girlfriend, who is a whore, is in the women's prison, and his father ended his days at the hands of a hangman in Valladolid, where he left a reputation for being a cruel and abrupt man.

When the good Chato causes an uproar in prison and the

mayor arrives to search the prisoners and look for *navajas,* he never finds any, even after ordering him to disrobe. [The *baratero*] knows how to hide it like no other, now attached with tar to the sole of the foot, now inserted in the anus, thus mocking the intelligence of the prison guard.

The *barateros* of the beach, if not as heartless as our Chato, are nonetheless of perverted intentions and tend to become killers in the jails and prisons. In reality, they do not differ in any way [from the other types], for in addition to sharing the same customs and concept of honor that has been formed among them, all *barateros* insist that they have honor; although for us their honor is as worthless as the one thieves derive from their villainous profession.

Crouching below the prow of a boat moored at the edge of the sea on the beach in Málaga, there are four or six rascals with their baskets at their side. A dirty and grimy deck of cards, which, due to its sticky state, is called *de arropiero*[9]—in Castile, *de turronero*[10]—is passed among them from one hand to another. The game that entertains them is called *ya el cané* or *ya el pecao*. On the sand there are some brass coins with which they wager.

Their look is anxious and fretful from fear of the unexpected arrival of a policeman[11] who, after clearing off their gambling table, may succeed in capturing one of them and hauling him off to jail. But no one appears in their surroundings and the game goes on with its appropriate blasphemies and interjections.

Suddenly and without [anyone] knowing how, [someone] pokes his head into the group; [he is] wearing a red cap that is somewhat discolored: the face of that head was swarthy, with axe-shaped sideburns, and large, hairy eyebrows. The above-mentioned head belongs to a tall, robust figure, around whose waist is tied a Moorish sash and on whose left shoulder is draped a red baize-lined jacket: it is a *baratero*.

"You see that," says the braggart, as he throws the group something covered in a brown paper previously used to wrap fried fish. It is a playing card.

One rascal from the group looks him in the face, picks up the card, and unwraps it for the killer, saying:

"Esteemed comrade, we don't need this."

"Young one," replies the hero of *El Perchél*,[12] "bring over the *barato*, and (taps his foot). . . .

The rascals pick up the money and get up, looking at the collector [i.e., the *baratero*] with a crafty and sarcastic air, like one of his own kind. The killer loses his temper, raises his hand, and tries to strike the rascals, but one of them leaps backward, draws a *navaja,* and, without wasting any time, strikes with a blow that lands the *baratero* on the ground.

Within a short time the waves of the ocean wash over the cadaver. . . .

But after two months have passed, a bell can be heard through the streets of the town, and the voice of a man saying: "Do good and offer Masses for the poor soul of one who is going to be executed."

The *barateros* of the beach.

To put a final touch on the preceding description, we attach below the beautiful composition by the distinguished poet Manuel Bretón de los Herreros.[13]

THE *BARATERO*[14]

He who murmurs dies by a blow
For I have bought the *baraja*[15]
Don't you know!
I have drawn my bare *navaja*
On novices and innocents, bestow
Your silver
It is I who collect the *barato*
At the *chapas* and at the *cané*
With rich tobacco and ripe wine
The life of a bishop is mine
Don't you know
My tastes are indulged every one
At my own expense there are none
And wherefore
Because I receive and never pay
At the *chapas* and at the *cané*.

MANUAL OF THE *BARATERO*

MANUAL DEL DISPARATERO

In *Sevillian Steel* I mention that the oldest extant treatise dedicated to the subject of knife fighting is *Manual del Baratero, o Arte de Manejar la Navaja, el Cuchillo, y la Tijera de los Jitanos.* Over the past few years, after acquiring facsimiles of the manual, a number of Western martial arts enthusiasts have attempted to "reconstruct" the "Spanish style of knife-fighting" by using this 57-page monograph as their bible.

The first obstacle such enthusiasts face is posed by the fact that most of them have little or no practical knowledge of the modern Spanish language, a minimal requisite to deciphering a work written in the Spanish of 150 years ago.

Some enthusiasts attempt to "solve" this language problem by enlisting the help of Spanish-speaking friends and/or significant others. Yet, even a fluency in Spanish is not sufficient. One has to be familiar with the written language of another era, much like when one first sets about to read the works of Chaucer or Shakespeare. Lacking such a familiarity leads to the obvious and inherent danger of assigning *literal* interpretations to words that held completely different meanings more than a century and a half ago.

A good example of this is the word *suerte*, which appears frequently in the manual. To the modern Spanish speaker it means "luck" or "fortune;" however, its meaning in 1849—now in disuse—was "tactic" or "ruse." Of course, the best example of this phenomenon is the word *baratero* in the manual's title, a term no longer used, since the "occupation" it refers to is no longer practiced.

Even the meaning of the word *manual* in Spanish is not identical to its meaning in English. A *manual* in the Spanish sense is not an instructional handbook (as it is in English), but merely a shorthand reference book to a larger body of knowledge that has already been mastered.

Beyond language fluency, the translator must have "fluency" in the basic principles of combat. A practical understanding of fighting in general, if not of knife-fighting, is necessary to understand the *context* of the writing. Even though most readers have this, the essential understanding of fighting principles is often missing when a second party is assisting with the translation.

Another common problem with some of the translations I have been requested to review is the literal translation of individual words instead of translating complete *idiomatic expressions*. Again, a practical familiarity with Spanish expressions is *de rigueur* for translation accuracy.

For example, in the manual's end essay, "*El Baratero*," the words "*cañería de pan*" can be individually translated as "piping of bread." In the same essay, the words "*armar un escándalo*" can be translated as " to arm a scandal." While such translations are meaningless, the knowledgeable person understands that the phrase "*cañería de pan*" is a term for throat or gullet, and "*armar un escándalo*" is used for "to cause an uproar."

And finally, even when the content of the manual is clearly understood, too many translators place undue importance on the content itself. They blindly overlook the fact that much of the manual's contents are *sociopolitical in nature* and contain little more than the most rudimentary of information.

Many have suggested that the author, Mariano de Rementeria, was quite likely a disenchanted member of the same "polite society" that he rails against. The overritualized fencing establishment of the time apparently maintained a snobbishness that excluded the "common man." It seems evident that the author felt victimized by his own exclusion from such fencing circles and that, in essence, the manual is a rant against Spanish fencing aristocrats. Its aims were to disparage the skills of the "sword aristocracy" by proposing that even knife-wielding Gypsy thugs are more accomplished than veteran fencers.

That notwithstanding, some enthusiasts have actually spent years—using Spanish-English dictionaries and Internet translation sites to plod through the morass of archaic terms—attempting to render the slim text into what they consider "intelligible" translations.

One misguided individual went so far as to attempt to translate the manual with the help of Hispanic acquaintances who knew as little as anyone else about 19th century Spanish idioms. The fact that the individual's ability to write articulately in English was as poor as his ability to translate Spanish resulted in an interpretation that was barely intelligible and almost wholly inaccurate.

I once happened to show Don Santiago a copy of one popular "English translation" that was posted on the Internet. After reading a few paragraphs of it, his keen wit quickly summed up its validity by quipping, "This translation should be retitled *Manual del Disparatero.*"[16]

NOTES

1. In the manual, *cañería del pan*.
2. In the manual, *corbatín de Vizcaya*. This was the Spanish term for the garrote method of execution, which was standard means used until as recently as 1974.
3. The dialect of the Spanish Gypsy.
4. In the military sense.
5. *Las chapas, la brisca, el cané, el pecao,* and *treinta y una* are all games of chance similar to "heads or tails." It was from such games that *barateros* exacted their commissions. In *chapas*, for example, the players gather in a circle, in the center of which are the *barateros*. The latter are charged with making certain that all coin tosses are clean and that players ultimately make good on their wagers. Each turn consists of tossing two coins. The player whose turn it is calls

either *caras* (heads) or *lises* (tails) before tossing his coins. The player wins or loses when *both* coins land either face up or down. If he wins, i.e., if the coins land as he called them, he wins the other players' wagers and repeats his turn. If he does not, he loses his wager and his turn, which then passes to the player to his right.

6. In the manual, *largo de uñas*, which means "long-nailed" and denotes a talent for stealing.

7. In a sarcastic sense.

8. The name assigned to the *baratero* in this story.

9. Syrupy; from *arrope*, or syrup.

10. Sticky; from *turrón*, a sweet nougat candy made from honey, egg whites, almonds, and hazelnuts.

11. In the manual, *aguacil*, which literally means dragonfly.

12. *El Perchél* is an old *barrio* in Málaga once noted for its dried-fish industry. Fresh fish from the adjacent Guadalmedina River were stacked, dried, and smoked on the *perchas*, or perches, from which the district derives its name. By night, however, *El Perchél*'s "industries" were pimping and gambling, as they were in similar towns throughout Andalusia. And, of course, wherever pimping and gambling took place, there were also *barateros* "working" to enforce the trade.

13. Manuel Bretón de los Herreros (1796–1873). Spanish poet and one of the most important and prolific comic playwrights of 19th century Spain.

14. Originally, after due consideration, I decided that there would be no point in translating Breton's original poem, not only because the translation would fail to rhyme, but also because the particular terms he uses are extremely obscure in meaning. Instead, I *completely* rewrote the poem in English, while attempting to keep to the tone of the original work. A few weeks later I discovered the current English translation hidden at the end of a chapter in Davillier's *Spain*.

15. Playing card.

16. The word *disparate* (DEES-pah-rah-teh) literally means "foolish talk," "nonsense," or "gibberish." A *disparatero*, then, is a speaker of foolishness, nonsense, and gibberish.

Afterword

This translation is written on paper, not in stone. I have received instruction in the Spanish knife arts, both formally and informally, since 1990; it was my immersion into these disciplines that emboldened me to prepare and render the present translation of *Manual del Baratero* for publication.

By the same token, not one year has gone by when I have not perfected an old skill, modified an existing belief, or learned a completely new method. As martial artists, we tend to become lifetime students. Although I originally translated this manual in 1995, the current translation reflects my enhanced understanding of its contents since that time.

That said, I have little doubt that over the next five or ten years I will have developed, or will be exposed to, newer, wider, and clearer understandings of this manual's contents. And just as the present work is a revised and expanded version of my original translation, so too will there likely be revisions, expansions, and perhaps even corrections to the present edition. And perhaps at that point it will be time for this translation to undergo its inevitable next revision.

In the meantime, reflect on the information presented here within the context of your current skill, for, as William Cassidy counseled many decades ago, "Respect for the practice of knife fighting breeds serious thought, and serious thought breeds better knife fighters."

Manual del Baratero

ó

Arte de Manejar la Navaja,
el Cuchillo, y las Tijeras
de los Jitanos

Prologo

Quizá habra algunos que al ver el presente Manual lo recibiran malamente, suponiendo perjudicial su aparicion, por ser la navaja el arma propia de los barateros, de los tahúres y de otras ciertas jentes de vida airada, las cuales deberían mas bien ignorar que apprender unos preceptos que redundarian en daño suyo, y por consiguiente en el de la sociedad.

A los que tal dijeren, podemos contestar manifestándoles que, cuando en esta sociedad hay ciertos males irremedia-

The Gipsy Rico

bles para los que no bastan los preceptos de la relijion, ni los tratados de la moral mas sublime, ni sirven las leyes, ni alcanzan nada las medidas mas eficazes; conviene adoptar un medio á fin de hacer que dichos males sean menos crueles, y en aleccionar á aquellos hombres honrados y pacificos que puedan verse acometidos inicuamente por los que hacen alarde de destreza en el manejo de las armas, y escudados con esta ventaja acuden al insulto y á la ofensa por la cosa ó palabra mas insignificante ó por puro placer de hacer daño.

Leyes represivas contra el duelo tiene la lejislacion española, tratando de estirpar esta bárbara costumbre que nos legaron los tiempos caballerescos, y en verdard que nada ha podido conseguirse; pues estamos viendo diariamente apelar á ese combate que llaman de honor á los hombres encargados precisamente de vijilar por el cumplimiento de las repetidas pragmáticas, órdenes y códigos que lo proiben.

No basta que haya personas intelijentes y virtuosas que se levanten contra los desafios, llamandolo el recurso de los *bribones y de los hombres inmorales*; y en vano se ha formado en otros paises mas ilustrados que el nuestro asociaciones respetables á fin de acabar con ellos, empleando todos los recursos que puede dictar el amor mas acendrado á la humanidad. El duelo continúa; y hemos visto *con escándalo* no hace mucho tiempo, que las leyes se desprecian por los mismos que las establecen.

"Guardaos," ha dicho Rousseau, hablando contra el duelo, "de confundir el nombre sagrado del honor con esa preocupacion feroz que pone todas las virtudes en la punta de una espada, y que sola es propia para hacer valientes infames. En que consiste esta preocupacion? En la opinion mas estravagante y bárbara que entró jamas en el espiritu humano, á saber, que los deberes de la sociedad se suplen con el valor; que un hombre no es picaro, bribon ni calumniador, y por lo contrario es politico, cortés, bien educado y humano cuando sabe batirse; que la mentira se trueca en verdad, en honradéz la perfidia, y se hace laudable la infidelidad en el momento que sostienen con el acero en la mano; que una afrenta queda reparada siempre bien por medio de una estocada; y que nunca se comete una sinrazon con un hombre con tal que se le mate."

Véase aqui un poco de lo mucho que se ha dicho contra el desafio, y sin embargo de todo no faltan en nuestros dias escritores que publiquen tratados apologéticos defendiéndolo, sin cuidarse que sus doctrinas estén en oposicion con las leyes. Qué demuestra esto? Le insuficiencia de dichas leyes, y el triunfo de las doctrinas de los duelistas.

Tolerado pues, el desafio, se hace necesaria la enseñanza del arte de manejar las armas para que sus efectos sean menos sensibles; ha habido una necesidad de instruir al débil para que sepa defenderse de las demasías del fuerte; y desde tiempos muy lejanos hay hombres que llevan el título pomposo de *Maestro mayor de los reinos*, otros que se dicen *Segundos tenientes*, y por ultimo los simplememte nombrados *Maestros de armas*, los cuales llaman á la coleccion de sus preceptos *El nobilisimo arte de la esgrima*.

Esos maestros de esgrima, ó de destreza, como se llamaban en lo antiguo, establezen sus *palestras* aun en los sitios mas públicos, y dan en ellas sus lecciones, sin que la autoridad, protectora de la vida de los ciudadanos, destruya esas cátedras de las cuales no han de salir sinó verdaderos homicidas; y véase aqui una contradiccion entre una ley que proibe el desafio, y otra que lo autoriza ó da carta de ecsamen á los preceptores públicos de florete.

Qué otra cosa son esos *asaltos* dados aun por personas del secso femenino, sinó escuelas, cuyos maestros enseñan á alcanzar triunfos con sangre humana? De qué hace alarde la llamada señorita Castellanos en sus sesiones de florete? De saber matar. Porqué se permite la enseñanza del tiro de la pistola? Porque hay ocasiones en que conviene usarla en defensa propia.

Luego, si aun conociéndose que es un mal atróz el desafio hay que tolerarlo, y conviene que se enseñe el modo de batirse; si nadie se escandaliza ni se levanta contra un tratado de esgrima, ni contra sus preceptos, antes por el contrario estos forman parte de la buena educacion de las altas clases, y no es uno cumplido caballero si no sabe empuñar un florete ó dar sablazos; si todo esto sucede, no hallamos razon para que alguno mirase con repugnancia la enseñanza de la navaja, y mucho mas cuando nos proponemos dar preceptos á los hombres honrados para que sepan usarla como arma defensiva.

Es indudable que no serían tan temibles ciertas jentecillas de navaja si se supiesen parar sus golpes; y una prueba de ello es, que cuando dos personas se desafian al florete, como ambas lo sepan manejar, por lo regular la pelea no suele traer funestas consecuencias. La navaja es un arma jeneralmente usada en España por la clase trabajadora, y nos choca sobremanera esa aversion con que la miran los que pertenecen á clases mas elevada. Aprendan pues á manejarla para ciertas ocasiones asi como aprenden el uso de las demás armas, y conocerán la utilidad de nuestro Manual. Si se nos dice que es el arma con que los barateros imponen la ley en los garitos y sacan la contribucion forzosa á los jugadores, diremos tambien que lo es del hombre honrado y pazifico que se encuentra acometido por un ratero, por un truan, y que no tiene otro medio de defense que ella y su corazon.

La navaja en fin, es el arma propia, como ya hemos dicho, de la clase trabajadora, del arriero, del trajinero, del artesano, del marinero, y un istrumento tan indispensable que muchos no pueden estar sin él. En vista de esto, vamos á fijar aqui las reglas necesarias para su mejor manejo en esos casos que se llaman de *honra*.

Además, si hay quien escriba tratados especiales de esgrima y del tiro de todas las armas para los caballeros, para los nobles, para los hombres de guante blanco y paletó, nosotros escribimos para el pueblo, para los hombres del pueblo, para esos de manos endurecidas y callosas á quienes los señores llaman *la canalla*, y sin la cual valdrian bien poco; y escribimos para los hombres del pueblo, porque estos tienen tambien sus desafios, casi siempre mas repentinos, mas bruscos, sin padrinos ni testigos, ni otras zarandajas ni panemas usadas en los duelos aristocráticos y de jente llamada decente.

Por último, escribimos tambien este Manual por si de nuestros conocimientos quieren valerse esos espadachines de profesion, los cuales aunque perfumados y vestidos de ricos trajes, están muy lejos de tener mejor conducta y moralidad que hombres de chaqueta y palo, y son muchas vezes mas dignos de castigo que los héroes de los garitos, entre quienes no es estraño encontrar rasgos particulares que están en contradiccion con su vida truanesca y peleadora.

~M.d.R.

INSTRUCCION
PARA MANEJAR LA NAVAJA

La instruccion para manejar la navaja se divide en cuatro partes.

La primera comprende el mecanismo del arma y las diferentes posiciones.

En la segunda se analizan las guardias, y se esplica el modo de acometer al contrario, dando una lijera idea de las varias suertes que se ejecutan, y de las tretas.

En la tercera se enseña el modo de manejar el cuchillo[1].

Ultimamente, en la cuarta se enseña el manejo de las tijeras entre los jitanos.

La primera parte se divide en once lecciones, la segunda en doce, le tercera en seis, y la cuarta en dos, del modo siguiente.

PRIMERA PARTE
Instruccion de la Navaja

Leccion primera:	De la navaja
Leccion segunda:	Sus Nombres Mas Usuales
Leccion tercera:	Posiciones ó Plantas
Leccion cuarta:	Modos de Acometer y Defenderse
Leccion quinta:	Del Terreno
Leccion sesta:	De los Jiros y Modos de Hacerlos
Leccion setima:	De los Contrajiros
Leccion octava:	Cambios
Leccion novena:	De los Golpes
Lecccion decimal:	De los Quites y Huidas
Leccion undecima:	De los Recursos

SEGUNDA PARTE
De las Varias Suertes que se Ejecutan al Jugar la Navaja

Leccion primera:	Guardias
Leccion segunda:	Golpes de frente
Leccion tercera:	Golpes de costado
Leccion cuarta:	Corridas
Leccion quinta:	Molinete
Leccion sesta:	Lanzar la Navaja
Leccion setima:	Pases de Mano y de Sombrero
Leccion octava:	Recortes
Leccion novena:	Suerte de la Culebra
Leccion decimal:	Engaños
Leccion undecima:	Tretas

TERCERA PARTE
Modo de Manejar el Cuchillo

Leccion primera:	Del Cuchillo
Leccion segunda:	Posiciones
Leccion tercera:	Golpes, Modo de Lanzar el Puñal
Leccion cuarta:	Quites y Huidas
Leccion qinta:	Recursos y Tretas
Leccion sesta:	Defensas del Cuchillo ó Puñal

CUARTA PARTE
El Manejo de las Tijeras entre los Jitanos

Leccion primera:	De las Tijeras
Leccion segunda:	Modo de Manejarlas entre los Jitanos

NOTES

1. Bajo el epigrafe de "Instruccion para manejar la navaja" comprendemos aquí el manejo del cuchillo y las tijeras, á fin de que encuentren mayor claridad los lectores.

Instruccion de la Navaja

LECCION PRIMERA
DE LA NAVAJA

Siendo la navaja un arma demasiado conocida en nuestro país, no cansaremos á nuestros lectores con una minuciosa esplicacion de su sencillo mecanismo. Bastará saber que las hay de diferented tamaños, y que no todas son a proposito para nuestro objeto.

En España hay varios pueblos notables por la buena calidad y temple que dan á las hojas de las navajas, siendo de admirar el agudo filo en

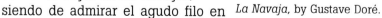

La Navaja, by Gustave Doré.

que rematan y que no se quiebra ni se tuerce despues de haber atravesado dos pesos duros ó una tabla del gueso de dos pulgadas. Albacete, Santa Cruz de Mudela, Guadij, Solana, Mora, Bonilla, Valencia, Sevilla, Jaen y otros muchos puntos tienen maestros de herreria, de cuyas manos salen obras mejor acabadas en ese jénero que las que puede producir el estranjero, y que recomendamos á los aficionados.

Pero como la figura de la navaja no siempre es adecuada para el uso que le habremos de dar en el curso de nuestra esplicacion, diremos que la hojá debera tener á lo mas un palmo de lonjitud, y estar perfectamente segura entre las cachas, prefiriéndose la navaja de muelle á otra cualquiera.

La figura de la hoja es de gran interés, pues no con cualquiera puede arriesgarse el diestro á tirar todo golpe indistintamente. Así, pues, sera la elejida de mucha panza ácia el estremo de la punta, teniendo de tres á cuatro dedos de latitud ó sea de anchura, y con punta algo prolongada, para dar *floretazos*; todo segun indica la presente figura.

LECCION SEGUNDA
DE LOS NOMBRES QUE RECIBE LA NAVAJA

La navaja recibe varios nombres entre las personas que la manejan. Nosotros no pondremos aquí todos, y si solamente los que se encuentran mas en uso, pues cada provincia le suele dar uno.

En Andalucia la llaman *la mojosa*, *la chaira*, *la tea*, y en Sevilla á la de mucha lonjitud *las del Santólio*; pero en los presidios y cárceles, y entre los barateros de Madrid y otros puntos es conocida con los nombres de *corte*, *herramienta*, *pincho*, *hierro*, *abanico*, *alfiler* y algun otro. En nuestras lecciones la llamaremos con el jeneral de navaja.

LECCION TERCERA
DE LAS POSICIONES O PLANTAS

El diestro en el manejo de la navaja tiene su primera posicion ó planta, del mismo modo que en el de la espada y sable, que se llama guardia. Despues de tomar la navaja con cualquiera de las manos colocando el dedo pulgar sobre el primer tercio de la hoja, cuyo corte deberá caer ácia la parte de adentro, se plantará en guardia á respetable distancia de su contrario mas bien lejos que cerca, con la mano desocupada pegada al cuerpo por la parte de la cintura y delantera del vientre, y en disposicion de recojer la navaja cuando se quiera hacer un *cambio*; los pies y piernas los colocara á igual distancia del contrario; un poco abiertas, y de modo de que le dé todo el cuerpo de frente, como se ve en le presente figura y de ningun modo de costado; á no ser que en alguna de las manos se use de sombrero, capa, chaqueta ó manta, en cuyo caso deberá colocarse con la pierna compañera del brazo en que esta el sombrero ó capa, ácia adelante y de manera que marca la figura que se halla en la leccion octava, de los *Cambios*.

Al caer en guardia se tendrá cuidado de recojer el vientre todo lo posible, para cuyo efecto habrá que encorvarse un poco, sin que por eso se saque demasiado la cara, pues se recibira un golpe en ella, y fuera muy vergonzoso. La vista estará siempre fija en la del contrario; de tal suerte que no variará de modo alguno, aunque éste trate de obligar á ello con engaños, palabras ó jestos; pues hay que advertir que el tirar bien á la navaja, consiste esencialmente en la lijereza de ojos y de pies, como iremos viendo en adelante.

LECCION CUARTA
MODOS DE ACOMETER Y DEFENDERSE

Despues que los combatientes se hallan colocados en su guardia, cuidará cada uno de no acometer de pronto á su contrario, y si esperar ser acometido por él para recibirle como es debido y conocer su destreza.

Para la intelijencia del mejor modo de atacar y defenderse, vamos á esplicar en las lecciones sucesivas lo que se entiende por *terreno*, *jiros*, *contrajiros* y *cambios*, palabras cuyo significado y conocimiento aos es indispensable.

LECCION QUINTA
DEL TERRENO

Llámase *terreno* el espacio comprendido en toda la estension del brazo y la navaja del diestro, dentro del cual solamente puede herir á su adversario.

Por lo tanto habrá dos *terrenos*, uno el terreno propio, y otro el terreno contrario.

LECCION SESTA
JIROS Y MODO DE HACERLOS

En los *jiros* estriba la mayor dificultad de este arte, necesitándose para hacerlos bien una admirable velozidad, que se adquiere con el mucho ejercicio.

Colocados los combatientes, uno enfrente de otro dejando entre sus *terrenos* el espacio de otro prócsimamente, hará el diestro el *jiro* para arrojarse sobre el contrario y alcanzar á herirle, adelantando insensiblemente ó de pronto uno de los pies y jirando el cuerpo de repente sobre su punta.

Cuando están en guardia los tiradores, no pueden llegarse á herir sin aprocsimarse, y el medio mas rápido y seguro de ejecutarlo es con un jiro que se podrá duplicar y triplicar, si el que los recibe huye el bulto.

Los jiros se hacen por el lado derecho y por el lado izquierdo.

Para hacerlos por el lado derecho, y por consiguiente para alcanzar al contrario por su costado izquierdo, será preciso avanzar con el pie izquierdo y jirar sobre él velozmente; hecho lo cual, si aquel no hace un *contrajiro* ó una *huida*, será herido indudablemente.

Para hacerlos por el lado izquierdo, se jira sobre el pie derecho, teniendo cuidado de colocar en el mismo instante la navaja en la mano izquierda con la que se ha de dar el *golpe*; si no es que ya estuviere anteriormente en dicha mano.

LECCION SÉTIMA
DE LOS CONTRAJIROS

Los contrajiros no son otra cosa que los mismos jiros que hace el diestro que es acometido que con uno de ellos, cuidando que sean al revés del que le hacen; es decir, si le viene un jiro por el lado derecho, jira sobre el pie del mismo lado, y huya el costado acometido ácia la parte de atrás, librándose así del golpe y pudiendo *atracar* á su contrario jeneralmente por la parte posterior del pecho.

El jiro es siempre avanzando, el contrajiro retrocediendo. De manera que un jiro tirado es destruido con un contrajiro, el cual es á su vez destruido con un segundo jiro, y este con un segundo contrajiro, y así sucesivamente; es la suerte mas bonita y de mejor perspectiva que presenta el manejo de la navaja. Véase el grabado anterior.

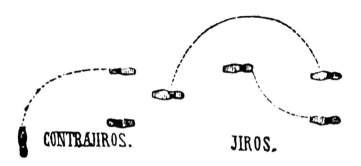

CONTRAJIROS.   JIROS.

LECCION OCTAVA
CAMBIOS

De los varios modos que hay de tirar á la navaja, es el mejor y mas seguro el que se verifica con ambas manos, es decir, pudiendo usar de cualquiera de ellas para su manejo, aunque algunos colocan en uno de los brazos la capa, manta ó chaqueta, ó bien el sobrero en la mano. Pero además de tener muy pocas ventajas esta manera de tirar, trae consigo muchas desventajas que deben tomarse en consideracion. Efectivamente, si atendemos á la facilidad con que puede variarse la vista del contrario con el sombrero en la mano, y al obstáculo que este presenta, á manera de escudo, á los golpes que vienen al diestro, seguramente que debiéramos adoptar como mas á propósito esta antigua costumbre de ponerse en guardia ó de tirar á la navaja; mas si nos detenemos á ecsaminar las muchas contras y hasta perjuicios que se siguen de no poder ejecutar los cambios ni acometer sino es por el lado de la mano armada, al mismo tiempo que la esposicion y riesgo en que se encuentra el diestro ó tirador en la guardia que ecsije esta manera de tirar, como representa esta figura, deduciremos sin duda alguna que el medio mas seguro y de mas recursos es usando de ambas manos para el combate, ó sea una mano armada y la otrá desarmada y libre, pero en diposicion de poderse armar tomando la navaja de la otra mano que quedará á su vez desarmada.

Es tal la velozidad que se necesita en esta suerte, que se llama *cambio*, que puestos en combate los dos tiradores, apenas la vista del uno puede penetrar en qué mano del otro se halla la navaja; y de aquí el no arriesgarse á acometer sinó con una lijereza mayor, que la que en igualdad de circunstancias se necesitaria para la otra manera de tirar que arriba hemos refutado.
No entiendan por eso

nuestros lectores que reprobamos en todas ocasiones el que el diestro ocupe una mano con el sombrero; por el contrario lo admitimos en algunos casos, considerando que es mas bien una suerte especial del arte, que una escuela aislada, sin embargo de ser tenida por tal entre algunos.

Para usar de esa suerte durante el combate, cuidará el diestro de no quitarse el sombrero de la cabeza y de que no caiga al suelo en las varias corridas y huidas que haga, con el objeto de apoderarse en ocasiones de él y colocarle en la mano desarmada, ó para arrojarle á los ojos del contrario ó finjirlo solamente, como mas adelante se dirá. Advertiremos de paso, que es de gran utilidad al diestro llevar faja á la cintura, ya para cubrir una parte del vientre y los vacios, y resistir de ese modo algun tanto por lo menos los *desjarretazos* y *viajes*, ya para ejecutar varias *tretas* con ella, y que en su respectivo lugar esplicaremos.

Cuando el diestro es citado ó provocado á reñir tendrá buen cuidado, si lleva capa, de arrojarla en sitio donde no pueda incomodarle enredándose entre sus pies; y de ningun modo reñira con ella colocada sobre los hombros, pues le estorbaria muchismo en sus movimientos, si bien la libertaria muchas vezes de ser herido; pero aconsejamos á los peleadores que abandonen siempre la capa.

La capa se puede abandonar con prontitud y de manera que no trabe las piernas del diestro. Esta suerte consiste en hacer un pequeño encojimiento de hombros, al mismo tiempo que un sacudimiento leve con la parte media de los brazos; y la capa queda tendída en tierra en forma de media luna ó abanico, en cuyo centro se encuentra colocado el tirador.

Este modo de libertarse de la capa sin riesgo de que se envuelvan los pies del diestro, tiene por objeto el no perder de vista al contrario, lo cual sucedería ciertamente si volviera la cabeza, como tendria que hacerlo para lanzar la capa fuera de su terreno; en cuyo caso se veía espuesto á ser acometido por su contrario aun antes que pudiera pestañear; debiéndose advertir que, por desgracia, no todos los que usan y manejan la navaja, tienen la jenerosidad y buena intencion que fueran de desear.

Hacemos esta advertencia porque, como indicamos en el prólogo, no es la aficion que podamos tener al arte de tirar á la navaja y el deseo de jeneralizar su enseñanza, lo que nos mueve á escribir este Manual; es solamente el que tenemos de que los ignorantes de su manejo, se pongan al corriente de las reglas para cuando se vieren acometidos por los que abusan de él, del mismo modo que abusarian de cualquier clase de arma.

Queremos destruir toda preocupacion, poniendo de manifiesto y al alcance de todas las personas, las diferentes suertes del arte y los medios, algunas vezes reprobados y de mal jénero, de que se valen los tiradores para reñir con los que no saben tomar la navaja en la mano. Con la lectura de esta *Instruccion* y una poca de práctica que facilmente se adquiere, podra cualquier almibarado señorito defenderse cuando menos del ataque mas brusco de un baratero.

LECCION NOVENA
DE LOS GOLPES

Colocados los tiradores uno enfrente de otro y con las navajas en mano, tratará cada uno de herir a su contrario, ó lo que es lo mismo, comenzarán á obrar las manos ó sean los *hierros*, con la ayuda de los movimientos de pies, que es lo mas esencial para dar los *golpes*.

Varias son las clases de *golpes* que pueden resultar de las diferentes posiciones y suertes que se ejecutan al tirar á la navaja; y reciben distinta denominacion segun la manera y sitio en que se dan, aunque todos están compredidos bajo la jeneral de *golpes* ó *puñaladas*.

Ante todo diremos que el cuerpo del diestro tiene dos partes que se llaman la *parte alta* y la *parte baja*.

Por *parte alta* se entiende todo el medio cuerpo comprendido desde la cintura hasta la frente inclusive.

Por *parte baja* se entiende todo el medio cuerpo comprendido desde la cintura hasta los pies. De manera que los golpes serán *altos* ó *bajos* segun que dén en la parle alta ó en la parte baja.

Si la *puñalá*, ó *mojá* como dicen los jitanos, se da en cualquier punto de la estension del vientre, se dice á esta suerte *atracar*, y al *golpe* se le llama *viaje*; así suele decirse entre los barateros "*vamos á echar un viaje*" por "*vamos á reñir ó á darnos una puñalada.*"

Cuando uno de los tiradores se arroja demasiado sobre el otro, este puede muy facilmente herirle solo con estirar veloz-mente el brazo y presentarle la punta del la navaja en la parte alta las mas vezes, cuyo golpe recibe el nombre de *floretazo*, y ninguno mas adecuado por la semejanza que guarda con la estocada que se dá con el florete en igual circunstancia, como se ve en las siguientes figuras.

No siempre el *floretazo* se da en la parte alta, pues hay una suerte, que ocupa el primer lugar entre mas seguras y de écsi-to mortal, que requiere ese mismo golpe en el centro de la *parte baja;*—el modo do hacerla se dirá oportunamente.

El *jabeque* ó *chirlo* es el golpe dado en la cara, el cual imprime en ella un sello de ignominia para los barateros; pues en efecto, de todos los golpes que en riña puede el diestro recibir, ninguno hay que con mas verdad manifieste su poca destreza, y revele el desprecio con que le ha tratado su contrario.

A la accion de herir en la cara se le llama *enfilar*.

El golpe dado en la parte alta y detrás de los vacios por

encima de las costillas, tiene por nombre *desjarretazo*; y es uno de los que prueban la habilidad del que le tira, abriendo algunas vezes con una ancha herida, la columna verlebral, llamada vulgarmente espinazo. Es mortal, y se da jeneralmente en los *jiros.*

Se entiende por *plumada*, el golpe ó puñalada tirado de derecha á izquireda describiendo jeneralmente una curva.

Llamase *revés* el golpe tirado con la mano vuelta ácia fuera y de izquireda á derecha.

La *plumada* y el *reves* segun van esplicados se entenderán tirados con la mano derecha; pues si lo fueren con la mano izquireda, la plumada será de izquierda á derecha, y el reves de derecha á izquierda.

LECCION DECIMA
QUITES, HUIDAS

Ya habrán conocido nuestros lectores que el arte de tirar á la navaja no está fundado en el solo capricho de algunos presidiarios ó jentes de mal vivir, y que está por el contrario, sujeto á reglas y principios tan esactos como los de la esgrima y el sable. Cuando lleguemos á hablar de algunas de las *tretas* que se usan en el manejo de la navaja, daremos la razon á los mas encarnizados detractores de esta arma, en lo que toca á aquellas, por ser su mayor parte nacida de las mas descuidada educacion y de los mas innobles sentimientos; pero hasta entonces, y prescindiendo de hechos que reprueban los hombres que se tienen en algo, sea de la clase que quiera, sostendremos que el arte de tirar á la navaja merece ser considerado del mismo modo que el de todas las otras armas.

Esplicados ya los medios de acometer, y las varias suertes *de golpes* mas dignas de atencion, vamos á dar ahora la esplicacion de los *quites* que estan en práctica para la defensa; parte muy esencial en todo manejo de arma blanca, pues sin ella sería nulo y de ningun valor cuanto se dijera relativo al modo de ofender.

Se cree por muchos que el medio mas seguro de tirar á la

navaja consiste en tener el cuerpo contínuamente en movimiento, suponiendo al diestro siempre brincando y siempre corriendo. Y nada hay seguramente con menos visos de verazidad: el diestro riñe con mucha calma y serenidad, y si bien salta grandes espacios y obra con prodijiosa lijereza, es cierto que lo ejecuta en ocasiones dadas y con muchísima oportunidad, moviéndose á vezes sin salir de un circulo de tres pies.

La serenidad hace al diestro ser oportuno en los movimientos, y ésta solo se adquiere con el mucho ejercicio; de tal suerte, que llega á acostumbrarse la vista á medir las distancias, y espera con tranquilidad y sin asustarse el golpe que le tira el contrario, cuando conoce que le ha de faltar una ó media pulgada para que alcance al cuerpo.

Si el golpe viene algo entrado en el terreno del diestro, se librará de el con encojer la parte del cuerpo amagada, y sin necesidad de huir ó brincar. Pero si la accion del contrario es para el diestro desconocida por su velozidad, ó el golpe que le tira se ha entrado hasta el centro del terreno, le esquivará con la huida brincando ácia atrás ó ácia un lado, á distancia suficiente para no ser alcanzado, y si pudiere ser, para alcanzar al que acomete; teniendo sumo cuidado de no caer sobre las plantas de los pies, y sí sobre las puntas con el objeto de no ser cojido en decuido y estar pronto para dar dos, tres, cuatro ó mas brincos.

Esta manera de *quitar* es la mas frecuente; pero hay otra que es mas arriesgada, aunque segura, si se acude á tiempo, y consiste en separar con el brazo desarmado el brazo armado del contrario cuando se aprocsima á herir. En los *floretazos* se ejecuta este *quite* con my buen écsito, llegando á vezes á cojer por la muñeca el brazo del adversario; por eso advertimos que aquellos golpes deben tirarse mur rápidamente y en disposicion de cortar la mano ó brazo que va á *quitar*, usando al efecto un *cuarto de plumada*.

Tirando con sombrero, se hacen los *quites* con él, intentando desarmar con un fuerte choque la mano que acomete.

Tambien se hace con frecuencia una suerte de quite, que es la mas arriesgada de todas, y es del modo siguiente.

Cuando el brazo armado del contarrio se aprocsima al terreno del diestro por la *parte baja*, este se libertará del golpe sacudiendole una recia patada en los dedos que sostienen la navaja, que se le hará soltar dejándole desarmado. Hemos dicho que es suerte arriesgada, y así es la verdad; pues si fallase al diestro el golpe intentado con el pie, seguramente seria herido por el contrario de una manera terrible, que solo podria remediar, arrojándose al suelo y dándole al mismo tiempo una patada en el bajo vientre.

LECCION UNDÉCIMA
RECURSOS

Cuando al diestro no son sufiecientes las reglas dadas para libertarse del contrario, ó para acometerle, tiene necesidad de apelar á los *recursos*; llamados así porque dan salida muchas vezes á lo que la destreza no ha podido hacer.

El arte de manejar la navaja ha establecido algunos que

esplicaremos muy por encima, por pertenecer su mayor parte á lo que con el nombre de *tretas* va comprendido en la segunda parte de esta Instruccion.

Bueno es saber que son los *recursos* un suple-reglas que alcazan á donde estas no; de aquí es que cada diestro pone en ejercicio los que mejor se le adaptan, ó los que él mismo ha inventado.

Daremos á conocer algunos *recursos*.

Pertenecen á la clase de *recursos*, los engaños ó *finjimientos* de que ya hablaremos.

El esconder el diestro sus dos manos detrás del cuerpo, para que el adversario no vea en cuál de ellas se halla la navaja, es un *recurso* de muy buen écsito, mayormente si al sacar la mano armada finje antes sacar la otra. Para hacer bien esta suerte bastará inclinar un poco el cuerpo por el lado del *engaño* y mover en la misma direccion el codo del brazo que engaña; pues el contrario se creerá acometido por aquella parte, y es muy natural que la huya, echando el cuerpo por la otra en la cual deberá recibir el golpe.

El dejarse caer en tierra con la naturalidad propia del que resbala, de modo que el contrario no sospeche que hay engaño, es un recurso, que bien ejecutado puede asegurar el fin que el diestro se propone; porque creyendo aquel que este ha caido involuntariamente, puede de buena fé arrojarse á el, el cual levantándose con presteza sobre una de las rodillas le recibe con la punta de la navaja hiriéndole en el bajo vientre, como representan las anteriores figuras. Es suerte que ecsije mucha lijereza en el diestro; de tal modo, que la hemos visto hacer dejando escapar al mismo tiempo la navaja para mejor engañar al adversario, y en el acto de incoporarse recojerla del suelo y á bastante distancia.

La *caida* suele hacerse de espalda; y el medio de levantarse es apoyando un pie y la mano desarmada fuertemente en tierra, y con lo restante del cuerpo, dando un violento empuje, situarse en la posicion dicha.

De las Varias Suertes que Se Ejecutan al Tirar á la Navaja

LECCION PRIMERA
GUARDIAS

Ya han visto nuestros lectores en la primera parte de esta Instruccion, y con la estension que cabe en un pequeño Manual como el presente, los principales medios de ofensa y defensa que tienen lugar en el ejercicio de la navaja; y decimos los principales medios, porque puede asegurarse que hay tantos como tiradores ó barateros, y fuera

Los Barateros, by Jose Luis Pellicer.

trabajo minucioso y dificil el dar una esplicacion completa de cada uno.

Conocidos, pues, los *golpes* y los *quites*, que son lo esencial á nuestro propósito, pasemos ahora á esplicar el modo de ponerlos en ejecucion, una vez colocados frente á frente los combatientes para reñir; es decir que e n s e ñ a r e m o s como ha de obrar el diestro segun la distinta *guardia* en que se ponga, y qué partido podrá sacar de los conocimientos adquiridos.

Es de tal manera notable lo mucho que la lijereza de ojos ayuda á toda clase de suertes, que estando en guardia el diestro puede aprocsimarse al contrario hasta tocar en su terreno, y por lo tanto arriesgarse considerablemente á ser herido, siempre que se proponga no permitirle mover el brazo armado; pues al mas insignificante movimiento que hiciese podria herirle en el mismo brazo, obligándole de esta manera á permanecer sin atacar. Esta suerte es de mucho peligro, porque para los dos combatientes solo hay un *terreno* donde ambos pueden herirse sin movimiento alguno de pies, y con estirar el brazo de la navaja.

El diestro se puede colocar en *guardia* usando de cual-

quiera de las *suertes*, pero con la espresa condicion de no olvidar un instante la posicion en que se encuentra, y de saber los puntos de su cuerpo espuestos al alcanze del brazo armado del contrario.

Hemos visto algunas vezes echarse en tierra al diestro, usando de esta suerte para *guardia* y es en verdad una de las mas seguras y en la que tiene mas probabilibades de no ser *atracado* sin riesgo inminente del contrario. El único medio facil de acometér al que se presenta en esta guardia es recibiendo sus golpes con el sombrero en la mano.

Siempre que el diestro acomete á su adversario tiene que hacerlo por la *parte alta* ó por la *parte baja*, como dijimos en su lugar; y de aquí se sigue, que cuando tira un golpe se arriesga á recibir otro en la *parte* contraria a la que acomete; es decir, que si tira á la *parte alta*, deja descubierta su *parte baja*, y si tira á la *parte baja* deja al descubierto su *parte alta*.

Se puede admitir como regla jeneral que el momento oportuno en que el diestro debe de herir á su contrario es aquel en que, despues de haber tirado este su golpe, retira el brazo armado que no pudo *hallar carne*, valiéndonos de una espresion que usan los barateros. Es menester mucho aplomo, y aguardar con cautel aquel momento que se aprovechará sin demora; y si no se lograre el objeto, hay que retirarse de pronto y lo mas bajo posible para no ser acometido á su vez en el instante de la retirada.

LECCION SEGUNDA
GOLPES DE FRENTE

Vamos ahora á esplicar las puñaladas que tienen lugar en las varias suertes que se ejecutan confundiendo los *terrenos*. Parecerá estrano á muchos de nuestros lectores el que no hayamos hablado de ellas, al tratar de las diversas especies de *golpes* que hemos esplicado en la primera parte de esta Instruccion; pero á esos les diremos, que preferimos esplicar en esta segunda parte los *golpes de frente* y de *costado* separadamente de todos los demás, porque despues de hablar en

la leccion anterior de las guardias, creemos deber hacerlo en esta y la que sigue, de los *golpes* que se tiran con los movimientos que se saben ya.

Por *golpes de frente* entendemos los que se tíran los combatientes cara á cara y sin buscarse los costados ni usar de *tretas*. Puesto en *guardia* el diestro, se vá aprocsimando á su contrario hasta confundir los *terrenos*, y entonces levantando con presteza el brazo armado le tira una *plumada* que llegará á herirle si no *huye* ó *quita*; lo que hará aquel estirando al mismo tiempo el brazo armado para dar un *floretazo*.

LECCION TERCERA
GOLPES DE COSTADO

Golpes de costado son los que se tíran los combatientes buscándose los vacios y las costillas, y se dan el los *jiros, contrajiros*, y muchas vezes en las *corridas*.

LECCION CUARTA
CORRIDAS

La *corrida* es una de las suertes mas usuales entre los *tiradores*; y podemos asegurar sin temor de equivocarnos, que es la mas esencial de este arte, ya porque en sí encierra todas las maneras de acometer al contrario, ó como se dice entre los barateros, de *buscarle el bulto*, ya de defenderse ó huir el cuerpo. En ella se tira toda clase de *golpes*, ó mejor dicho, es el arte completo.

La *corrida* no es otra cosa que la descripcion de un semicirculo hecho por cada uno de los combatientes en el acto de la riña; pero procurando siempre conservar la primitiva distancia hasta que llegue el momento de acometer, en cuyo caso habrá necesidad de entrarse en el terreno contrario y herir con cualquiera de los golpes conocidos.

La *corrida* se ejecuta marchando por uno de los lados indistintamente y sin variar la primera posicion de la guardia, unas

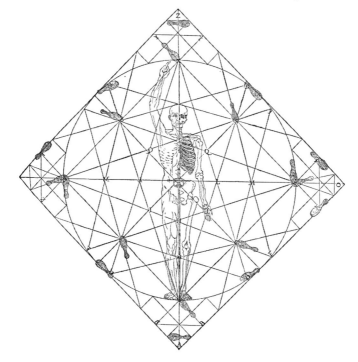

vezes por la izquireda otros por la derecha; pues siempre que uno de los *tiradores* ataca al otro, el acometido *jira* ó *huye* con la *corrida* por el lado opuesto, ó se sale del *terreno* brincando. De aquí resulta que los dos semicirculos que forman los combatientes, uno enfrente del otro, llegan á describir un circulo entero, mas ó menos perfecto, y de una variada visualidad.

Cuanta mayor lijereza tenga el diestro en sus pies, tanto mejor se ejecutara la *corrida*, porque como ya dijimos, este arte estriba mas en la ajilidad y sangre fria del diestro que en ninguna otra cosa; pues aunque el uso es muy esencial, de nada serviria sin el ausilio de esas dos cualidades.

LECCION QUINTA
MOLINETE

Cuando el contrario se arroja demasiado sobre el diestro, deberá este usar del *molinete*, que consiste en levantar del suelo uno de los pies, y sobre el otro jirar todo el cuerpo en derredor con mucha velozidad, y parándole de pronto, estirar el brazo armado para dar un *floretazo* al que le acomete.

Téngase presente que es suerte muy peligrosa, y que la ocasion mas oportuna para ejecutarla es cuando el adversario tira el *golpe* por bajo, no debiendo hacerse cuando el golpe viene por alto; pues ya hemos dicho que el floretazo se tira casi siempre á la *parte alta*, y para ello se necesita que el golpe del contrario amague á la *parte baja*.

Si el diestro se halla muy *cerrado* por su parte alta, es decir, si es acometido por el contrario muy dentro del *terreno propio*, le recibirá bajando el cuerpo hasta colocarse con una rodilla en tierra y presentándole la navaja ácia el bajo vientre. Véase la figura de la leccion undécima, parte primera.

Tenemos que advertir que tanto en el *molinete* como en los *floretazos* altos se espone el diestro á que le coja su brazo armado, el brazo desarmado del adversario, quien volviéndole con fuerza su muñeca ácia la garganta podrá herirle con su misma navaja.

LECCION SESTA
LANZAR LA NAVAJA

Entre muchos *tiradores*, y mas comunmente entre los marineros, se acostumbra lanzar la navaja al cuerpo del contrario, la cual llevan sujeta á la cintura con un largo cordon ó cadenilla de alambre.

Parecerá incredible á algunos de nuestros lectores la prodijiosa punteria con que hemos visto lanzar la navaja, dejándola clavada en el pecho ó vientre, y precisamente en el punto que la vista del diestro habia señalado; pero nada hay mas cierto, y tan admirable habilidad solo es comparable con la que manifiesta aquel á quien la navaja se dirije, llegando en muchos casos á libertarse del *golpe*, y hasta cojer el cordon que la sujeta y cortarle con la suya.

Nosotros á la par que admiramos tanta ajilidad y destreza, aconsejamos á los tiradores que nunca usen de esta suerte por lo incierto y peligrosa que es; á pesar de haber hombres que la ejecutan con tal acierto, y que solo debe atribuirse al continuado ejercicio que en ello tienen desde muchachos.

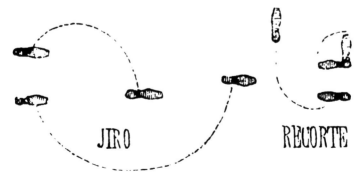

JIRO   RECORTE

LECCION SÉTIMA
PASES DE MANO Y DE SOMBRERO

Puesto que ya hemos visto que la lijeza y prontitud de la vista es lo que mas contribuyen al buen manejo de la navaja, esplicaremos el medio de que se valen los tiradores para obligar al contrario á variarla ó á cerrar los ojos. Despues que el diestro ha finjido ó tirado algunos golpes, y quiere desviar la vista del adversario para acometerle; en el mismo momento que lo hiciere, ó bien se pasará la mano desarmada por delante de los ojos ó por los de aquel, ó bien tomando el sombrero que llevará en la cabeza lo pasará una ó mas vezes de la misma manera, en cuyo instante se arrojará sobre él por la *parte baja* á herirle en el vientre.

LECCION OCTAVA
RECORTES

El *recorte* no es mas que un *jiro*, con la diferencia de que el diestro al ejecutarlo da la espalda al contrario, mientras que el *jiro* requiere que se haga dando siempre el frente.

Tiene lugar cuando el diestro es acometido con un *jiro* ácia el espinazo, y es muy espuesto.

LECCION NOVENA
SUERTE DE LA CULEBRA

La suerte de la *culebra* consiste en arrojarse de pechos al suelo el diestro que la va á ejecutar, y apoyado en la mano desarmada ir andando ácia el terreno del contrario á herirle en su bajo vientre con *floretazo* ó *plumada*.

LECCION DÉCIMA
ENGAÑOS

Todo *golpe* puede ser verdadero ó finjido.

Se llama verdadero, cuando la intencion del que le tira, es herir á su adversario.

Es finjido, cuando el diestro lo marca solamente con el fin de engañar y cojer desprevenido á su contrario.

Así, pues, en las *puñaladas de frente*, se finjirá el golpe á la parte baja, para poder herir con acierto en la *parte alta*, y vice versa; pues amagado el diestro por alto acudirá naturalmente al mismo punto con su navaja, si no conoce el engaño, y quedará descubierto por lo bajo á donde irá el golpe verdadero; y amagado por lo bajo acudirá allí con su mano armada, yendo entonces el golpe á lo alto y jeneralmente á *enfilar*.

Se puede establecer por regla jeneral, que todo golpe verdadero puede convertirse en *golpe finjido* ó sea *engaño*, y todo golpe finjido convertirse en golpe verdadero.

Se pueden igualmente finjir los jiros y contrajiros, y así el diestro, por ejemplo, hará uno finjido por cualquier lado, con el cual, engañado su contario hará el contrajiro correspondiente, presentando de este modo descubierto el lado á donde irá el golpe verdadero.

LECCION UNDÉCIMA
TRETAS

Hemos llegado al punto en que con razon nos pondremos de parte de los que aborrezen el manejo de la navaja. Seguramente que si no atendiesemos á otra cosa que á lo que resulta del uso de algunas *tretas* que ponen en practica ciertos tiradores, debiéramos acusar de inmoral y altamente innoble su ejercicio; pero ya han visto nuestros lectores las reglas fundamentales que hemos dado en el curso de nuestras lecciones, y conocerán que no todo en el arte de tirar á la navaja es vil y reprobado, y que por el contrario se le debe considerar sujeto á principios jenerales como el de cualquiera otra arma. No quisiéramos nosotros que, por la relacion de varias *tretas* de que se valen muchos hombres degradados y cobardes, se formase una idea equivocada de los *tiradores* de navaja, cuando el abuso que de ella hacen aquellos no pertenece al arte; los que así obran con la navaja obrarian del mismo modo con un florete ó con un sable. Por lo tanto nos abstenemos de indicarlas por lo repugnantes que aparecen á nuestros ojos, y por lo distante que están del objeto que nos propusimos al escribir este *Manual;* mas no nos es possible al mismo tiempo prescindir de hablar de algunas que creemos adaptables en casos de apuro, ó que conviene que las evite el hombre acometido injustamente.

Ya hemos dicho en la primera parte, que con la faja que el diestro debe llevar á la cintura se ejecutan algunas tretas, y así es la verdad. En las varias *corridas* que se hacen en riña, cuando el diestro quiere practicar una treta con su faja, no tiene mas que soltar el estremo de ella y dejarla arrastrar por el suelo, de manera que su contrario facilimente la pise, en cuyo caso tirando velozmente de ella le hará caer en tierra ó tropezar malamente.

Otra treta se ejecuta con la faja, y es: llevando en el estremo de ella dinero, piedras, ó cualquier cosa que la haga bastante pesada, la arrojará el diestro con violencia á las piernas de su adversario, el cual se encontrará trabado y sin poder moverse, quedando en disposicion de ser herido.

El sombrero se arroja á la cara del contrario, y es treta de muy buen efecto.

Algunas vezes el diestro recoje un puñado de tierra, si en el lugar de la riña la hubiere, y le tira á los ojos del adversario, yéndole á *atracar* sin demora.

El diestro puede tambien pisar con uno de sus pies otro del contrario, y es treta de buen écsito si no se evita.

Puede tambien el diestro dar á su contrario una fuerte patada en el vientre, ó enredar con sus piernas las de aquel, haciéndole dar en tierra.

El diestro puede desviar su vista de la del contrario, y dirijirla ácia la parte de atrás de éste, el cual creyendo que mira á alguno que está á su espalda, vuelve la cabeza y en el punto es *atracado.*

"Tente, que vas á tropezar" dice el diestro á su contrario, con el objeto de que se dirija á mirar al suelo, y en el acto le hiere.

Por último, son tantas las tretas que emplean los tiradores, que se necesitaria mucho tiempo para esplicarlas todas; y así nos contentamos con haber puesto las mas comunes y jenerales.

Modo de Manejar el Cuchillo

Fencing with the Puñal, by Gustave Doré.

LECION PRIMERA
DEL CUCHILLO

Pocos tenemos que decir del *cuchillo* ó *puñal*, estando su manejo sujeto en la mayor parte á las reglas que hemos dado para tirar á la navaja. Solamente tendremos que advertir, que los golpes del cuchillo son siempre de punta, y que no reciben otro nombre que el de *puñaladas*.

MANUAL DEL BARATERO

El cuchillo lo usan mucho los marineros; y en las cárceles y presidios es arma con la que cobran el barato frecuentemente los matones.

LECCION SEGUNDA
POSICIONES

La planta mas segura para manejar el cuchillo ó puñal es la que representan las figuras de la pájina siguiente. El cuchillo se toma con la mano derecha y de la manera que major acomode al diestro; en el brazo izquierdo se lia la capa, chaqueta ó manta, ó bien se coloca, como lo hacen los barateros, una red de cañas ó un cuero de bastante resistencia, con lo que se paran las puñaladas y se cubre la vista del contrario. La planta no es la misma que se usa en el tiro de navaja, pues en el manejo de cuchillo se coloca el diestro con el brazo y la pierna izquierda sacados al frente del contrario.

A falta de otra cosa con que cubrir el brazo desarmado se usa poner el sombrero ó gorra en la mano. Por lo demás es igual en un todo á lo que se ha dicho para la navaja.

LECCION TERCERA
GOLPES, MODO DE LANZAR EL PUÑAL

Los golpes con el cuchillo ó puñal se dan siempre con una mano, es decir, que no hay *cambios*, y por lo mismo van dirijidos ácia el lado desarmado del contrario, cuidando de herir en el costado izquierdo, que es lo mas seguro.

Los *jiros* tambien se ejecutan con muy buen écsito, aunque solamente tienen lugar los del lado derecho, como igualmente el *contrajiro* izquierdo.

El cuchillo se lanza al cuerpo del contrario estendiéndose sobre la palma de la mano y con el mango ácia fuera; y asi puesto, se arroja con impetus y se lo clava, á no ser que huya el cuerpo brincando ó echándose en tierra.

LECCION CUARTA
QUITES, HUIDAS

Los *quites* y las *huidas* son esactamente iguales á los del manejo de la navaja; —obsérvese lo que va esplicado en aquel lugar.

LECCION QUINTA
RECURSOS Y TRETAS

Véase lo que dijimos al hablar de los *recursos* y *tretas* de la navaja.

LECCION SESTA
DEFENSAS DEL PUÑAL

Si en alguna ocasion se encontrase el diestro sin cuchillo, como suele suceder, y se le presentase uno de los muchos hombres que hay de mala intencion con un puñal ó cuchillo en la mano, en este caso no ha de huir, pues le estará mal; lo que debe hacer es esperarle en guardia de sombrero por el lado

derecho, pero sin él y con el brazo levantado, de manera que la mano esté aun mas alta que la cabeza, descubriendo todo el pecho, como lo manifiestan las siguientes figures; y cuando el contrario le tire la puñalada, se defenderá el diestro dándole con la mano un golpe en la muñeca, y si puede ser agarrándosela por debajo; y si no, no desunirse, y al mismo tiempo huir el pie izquierdo formando con el cuerpo concavidad, y levantando el derecho para sentarle detrás del izquierdo de su contrario; haciendo centro en el izquierdo, le echará la mano izquierda al cogote, procurando hacer todos los movimientos sin temor, y muy prontos, y se logrará la defensa. Y si hallándose el contrario en esta disposicion por haberle salido fallida su resolucion, se fuese á retirar para volver á acometer, el diestro en aquel mismo tiempo le ayudará á levantar, empujándole para que su mismo instrumento le sea en su perjuicio.

El Manejo de las Tijeras entre los Jitanos

LECCION PRIMERA
DE LAS TIJERAS

Los jitanos son los únicos que manejan esta clase de arma, sin duda porque jeneralmente dedicados al trafico y comercio

Duel with the Santólios, by Gustave Doré.

de caballerias la llevan consigo para esquilar las mulas y pollinos. Hay tambien esquiladores aragoneses. Escusamos describir aquí su mecanismo, pues ninguno de nuestros lectores dejará de conocerle.

LECCION SEGUNDA
MODO DE MANEJARLAS

El modo de manejar las tijeras en riña, es igual al del cuchillo que ya hemos esplicado; y solo tenemos que añadir que, cojidas por el centro que forman sus cuatro patas cuando están abiertas, la herida que causan es comunmente con las dos puntas, y siempre mortal.

Nada mas tenemos que decir del manejo de esta arma que no vaya dicho en el de la navaja y en el del cuchillo, teniendo en ella lugar su aplicacion, y siendo las reglas communes á las tres armas.

El Baratero

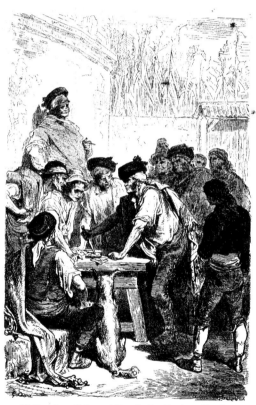

El Baratero Cobra el Barato, by Gustave Doré.

Tipos sumamente particulares tiene España que puede decirse no se encuentran semejantes ni aun parecidos en otras naciones; pero ninguno tan marcado como el baratero, ó sea el maton que saca un impuesto forzoso en los circulos de los tahúres que se llaman garitos. Este personaje truanesco nacido regularmente de la hez del pueblo, y criado en las cárceles y presidios, tiene con frecuencia un fin trájico, acarreado por sus azañas ya sea en medio de una playa ó de un hejido á manos de otro mas valiente ó mas afortunado que él, que le *arrebaña* el mondongo ante un público formado de charranes, soldados, ladrones y *gachés*; ya en el centro de una plazuela ó escampado, encima de un tablado de alguna elevacion y á manos del ejecutor de la justicia, el cual despues del ¿me perdonas? consabido, le aprieta y descompone *la cañeria del pan* con el mayor desenfado del mundo, aplicándole al cuello un *corbatin de Vizcaya*.

Tres son pues, las clases de barateros conocidos: el baratero de tropa, el de la carcel, y el de la playa; y vamos á hablar de ellos separadamente.

El *baratero de tropa*, educado en los cuarteles y cantinas donde hizo su trabajoso aprendizaje, es conocido en el acto por su aire ternejal y de perdona-vidas, su apostura maja, siempre con un *pitoche* ó cigarro en la boca y otro sostenido en la oreja, pelo mas largo que todos los soldados de su compañia, la gorra de cuartel ladeada, la casaca sin abotonar por el pecho, y el cuello de ella doblado ácia afuera, una mano en el bolsillo del pantalon y la otra colocada sobre la cadera y enseñando en el dedo meñique un anillo de laton; escupe por el colmillo y habla andaluz y *caló*, es muy moreno, casi siempre feo, y si es bizco, mejor; lleva el bigote unas vezes corto, y otras retorcido á lo borgoñon; habla guiñando el ojo y meneando una pierna. Es el *temeron* de la compañía, y el sarjento primero le releva de la mecánica del cuartel, porque en ocasiones necesita dinero, y el baratero le franquea su bolsillo, que está repleto, merced á las trampas y puñaladas en que es tan entendido, y le han alcanzado alto renombre y gran *poer* entre sus *camarás*. El *baratero* de la compañía es el mas holgazan de ella, sabe mal el ejercicio y desprecia completamente la ordenanza; pero en cambio maneja como ninguno la *herramienta*, juega á las *chapas* y á la brisca, al cané, á la treinta y una, bebe y triunfa, tiene moza, que es la cantinera del cuartel, y se hace obedecer de todos. En tiempo de campaña se bate como el primero, porque es valiente, y no queda el ultimo para el *pillaje*, porque es largo de uñas.

En los pueblos donde pára, busca los garitos, y en ellos hace sus ensayos entre la jente mas perdida con quien se relaciona amistosamente, la cual suele pagar su cariño y simpatias con una paliza ó un par de puñaladas, que alcanza por alguna *fullería* no muy limpia.

Este baratero es enemigo nato de los paisanos, á quienes llama patrones; por un quitame allá esas pajas mete mano al primero que topa y que él cree le ha *diquelado* con malos *clisos*, y arma un zipizape de todos los diablos. El coronel se entera del escándalo y le mete en un calabozo, del que sale á los dos dias mas *terne y echao pa alantre* y en disposicion de *armarla* con *cualsiquiera*. Pega una paliza diaria á su querida, y la abandona por la del cabo furriel, que se viene con él, y á quien corta la *fila* á la primera infidelidad que le hace.

Cuando el rejimiento pernocta en alguna poblacion, es visitado el *baratero* de cada compañía por los barateros que hay allí, que muchas vezes son desertores de presidio que se hallan ocultos sin *olfatearlo* la justicia; se llaman *camaráas ó compares*, y van á beber juntos unas copas ó *cañitas* que se tiran á la cara á la mas pequeña contradiccion ó jesto desabrido; se salen á la calle, y empuñando los *alfileres*, se tiran dos ó tres *mojadas* que sirven para que la amistad eche entre ellos hondas raizes; se presentan mútuamente en los garitos en que *mandan* ó *comen*, pero con la espresa condicion de no *inquietar* á *naide*, ni querer cobrar los *chavos* donde los cobra su *camará*.

Sigamos con el *baratero de la carcel*. Este es del jénero mas temido de todos. De muchacho ha sido matachin, en cuyo oficio aprendió todos los modos de *destripar*; las horas que tenia libres, que eran las mas, se entretenia en saquear los bolsillos del prójimo elegante, ó de cualquiera que le deparaba la suerte indistintamente; conocia á la primera ojeada al patan ó paleto; engañabale bajo cualquier pretesto y le *espantaba* los *parnées*, sin que lo advirtiera, los cuales iba á jugar al cané con otros muchachos á quienes ganaba lo que tenian, á fuerza de trampas y de amenazas obscenas. Si á pesar de todo era él el perdidoso, allí de su jenio y sus manos, tiraba del pincho y lograba que á la fuerza le entregáran sus caudales, lo cual le iba dando nombradia entre los pilletes y *gatería* de la ciudad. Asi fué aumentando en años y picardias, dejando el pabellon bien puesto en las tabernas, cárceles y garitos, donde su fama era colosal. Por ultimo, sentada ya su reputacion, y haciéndose temer de todos los ternejales del matadero, lo llevaron por vijésima vez al *estarivél* sus fechorias y mala lengua. Puesto en él, no se contentó con una posicion brillante entre los presos, sinó que aspiró á mas y lo alcanzó: estaban jugando en el patio á las chapas como una veintena de ellos, y mi hombre llega al corro, tose de una manera particular, y con voz ronca y sosegada pregunta, mirando de reojo á una enorme navaja que estaba hincada en el suelo:

"*¿De quién es esa friolera?*"

Mia, repuso el dueño de ella con un jesto que daba horror, y *naide come aquí sinó yo*.

Pues, camará, me jace mal al estómago y la quiéo gomitar; y dándola con el pie la hizo rodar un buen trecho por el suelo.

Allí fué Troya, ánimas benditas! El que cobraba los *chavos* defendió valientemente su derecho adquirido, pero no tanto que mi *Chato* (algun nombre le habremos de dar), entrándole la *herramienta* por el vientre, no le echára el cuajar al aire con grande admiracion de tan honrados circunstantes. Desde entonces es el *baratero* de la carcel y nadie le tose, cumpliendo con su deber sin que mala *mui* le quite la honra.

¿Quereis, lectores curiosos, conocer al buen *Chato* entre aquella multitud que se rebulle en el patio? Mirad, allí á la derecha, entre aquel corro de pelgares….ya dísteis con él. Su estatura es mas bien pequeña que alta, ancho de espaldas, la fisonomía repugnante y estúpida, muy moreno, grandes patillas y largos tufos sobre la frente que lleva recojidos ácia un lado, y algo caidos sobre la ceja izquierda. Su traje está en completea proporcion con su figura; ancho pantalon de pana verde sostenido en la cintura por una disforme faja de estambre, que es á la vez su pequeño maletin en donde guarda los dineros, la *tea* y la baraja; calza alpargatas ó borceguíes de becerro bastante grotescos; está comunmente en mangas de camisa, y lleva atado al rededor de la cabeza un pañuelo de yerbas que le dá un aspecto siniestro y horripilante. Escusado es decir que su querida, que es una *lúmia*, está en la galera, y su padre concluyó sus dias á manos del verdugo de Valladolid, en cuyo canal dejó fama de hombre de *malas tripas* y *mu campechano.*

Cuando el buen Chato arma un escándalo en la *Casa de poco trigo*, y llega á entrar el alcaide para rejistrar á los presos y buscar las navajas, jamás se la encuentra, aunque le mande desnudar. Sábela esconder como ninguno, y pegada con pez en la planta del pie, ya metida en el ano, burlando así la sagazidad del calabozero.

Los *barateros de playa*, si bien no tan desalmados como el Chato, son sin embargo de intenciones perversas, y suelen llegar á ser matones de las cárceles y presidios; pues en realidad en nada se diferencian, siendo unas las costumbres y una la idea del *honor* que ellos se han formado, que tambien los barateros dicen que tienen *honor*; aunque para nosotros su honor vale tanto como el que sacan los ladrones de su villana profesion.

Agachados debajo de la proa de un falucho barado á la orilla de la mar en la playa de Málaga, se hallan cuatro ó seis charranes con sus cenachos al lado: una barajilla sucia y mugrienta, que por su estado pegajoso suelen llamarla allí de *arropiero*, y en Castilla de turronero, corre de mano en mano. El juego que los entretiene se llama ya el cané ó ya el *pecao*. En la arena hay algunos cuartos de los que *meten*. Su mirar es inquieto y zozobroso, porque temen la llegada repentina de un alguacil, que arrebañando *la mesa* consigue además cojer á alguno y dar con él en la carcel. Pero en los *alreores* no se dica ninguno, y el juego continua con sus blasfemias é interjecciones correspondientes.

De pronto y sin saber cómo, se asomó al corro una cabeza que llevaba calado un gorro encarnado algo descolorido: la

MANUAL DEL BARATERO

cara de aquella cabeza era atezada, tenia unas patillas de *boca de jacha*, grandes y pobladas cejas. La susodicha cabeza pertenecia á un cuerpo alto, robusto, en cuya cintura se liaba una faja moruna, y de cuyo hombro izquierdo pendia una chaqueta forrada de bayeta encarnada; era un baratero.

Ahí va eso, dijo el jaqueton tirando al corro una cosa liada en un papel de estraza en que antes se habia envuelto pescado frito; era una baraja.

Uno de los charranes le mira al rostro, recoje los naipes y se los devuelve al maton, diciéndole:

Estimado, camará, nojotros no nesesitamo jeso.

Chiquiyo, le repone el héroe del Perchél, venga aquí el barato, y . . . sonsoniche!

Los charranes recojen los chavos y se levantan mirando al *cobraor* con aquel aire pillesco y zumbon, propio de los de su clase. Al maton se le *ajuma el pescao*, alza la mano y *quié pegales*, pero uno de ellos da un salto atrás, desembucha una tea, y sin andarse en piquis miquis, zás! le pega un metio que da con el baratero en tierra.

Las olas del mar bañan á poco rato un cadaver. . . .

Pero pasado unos dos meses, se oia por las calles de la poblacion una campanilla y la voz de un hombre que decia: "para hacer bien y decir misas por el alma de un pobre que van á ajusticiar."

Los barateros de la playa.

A fin de perfeccionar el cuadro anterior, trasladamos aquí la linda composicion del distinguido poeta don Manuel Breton de los Herreros, titulada

EL BARATERO

Al que me gruña le mato,
Que yo compré la baraja:
¿está osté?
Ya desnudé mi navaja:
lárgue el coscon y el novato
su parné,
Porque yo cobro el barato
en las chapas y el cané.

Tiemblan sarjentos y cabos
cuando me pongo furioso:
¿está osté?
En donde yo campo y toso
no hay ternejales, no hay bravos.
¡chachipé!

porque yo cobro los chavos
en las chapas y el cané.
A naide temo ni envidio:
soy mu feroz y mu cruo:
¿está osté?
Y si la ley del embuo me echa mañana á presidio,
yo sabré
cobrar en Seuta el susidio
de las chapas y el cané.

Rico trujan y buen trago. . . .
!tengo una vida de obispo!
¿está osté?
Mi voluntá satisfago
y á costa ajena machispo,
?y por qué?
Porque yo cobro y no pago
en las chapas y el cané.

Así camelo y recluto
el corazon de mi mosa:
¿está osté?
Y aunque ha peinao corosa,
sere su rey asoluto:
lo seré!
mientras me paguen tributo
en las chapas y el cané.

APPENDIX A

The Language of the *Baratero*

It becomes clear when reading *Manual del Baratero* in the original language that a majority of the terms associated with the art of handling the *navaja* possess a distinctive Andalusian pronunciation, if not provenance. The prevalence of these terms lends credence to the popularly held belief that southern Spain was the cradle of Mediterranean knife arts.

The innumerable linguistic traits and customs that distinguish the Andalusian form of speech from Castilian and other Spanish dialects have been catalogued in volumes of sociolinguistic studies and lie outside the realm of this translation. One notable linguistic trait, however, is the Andalusian suppression of the intervocal *d* sound, i.e., the *d* occurring between two vowels. This proclivity, frowned upon by most speakers of "proper" Spanish, accounts for the use of such regional pronunciations as *mojá* (for the proper *mojada*) and *puñalá* (for *puñalada*) in the manual. These and many other idiosyncrasies of the Andalusian dialect occur as frequently in the text as they do in actual speech.

Aside from the marked Andalusian flavor of many words, the language of the traditional *navajero* also harbors influences from three other distinct elements of Spanish culture. The first is the vernacular of traditional Spanish fencing, or *Destreza*, as it was historically known. From *Destreza*, *navajeros* borrowed such terms as *diestro, contrario, floretazo*, and so forth.

The second linguistic influence on the *navajero's* language was the art of bullfighting, locally known as *toreo*. Not only is *toreo* a major cultural aspect of Spanish life, but its protagonists—*picadores, toreadores*, and *matadores*—also use an edged weapon for the killing of their "opponent," the bull. The *navajero* has coopted words such as *enfilar, suerte*, and *terreno* from the jargon of *toreo*. Apart from these there are various other words, not necessarily found in the manual, that have likewise been borrowed from *toreo*, among them *veronicas, atravesada, pinchazo, metisaca*, and so on.

The third domain of linguistic influence, previously discussed, is from *germania*, the old language of the criminal subculture. While *germania* is no longer spoken today, many of the terms taken from it remain in contemporary use.

Contrary to what one might expect in a work purporting to portray elements of Gypsy culture, there are very few words from the caló or Romany dialects in the manual. In fact, while many of the ruses described are suspected to be of Gypsy origin, the language of the text, with the exception of a few words, is exclusively Spanish.

The common caló equivalents for *navaja, cuchillo*, and *tijeras* are *serdañi, churi*, and *cachas*, respectively, but the author uses the more mainstream Spanish terms. I found this especially surprising given the amount of Gypsy terms that permeate the *navajero* vernacular and the existence of caló-Spanish dictionaries at the time of the original date of publication. Evidently, Mariano's eminent linguistic abilities did not extend to the language of the "*jitanos*" whose methods he writes about.

THE *NAVAJERO* LEXICON

To assist the reader in his understanding the world of *navajeros* and *barateros*, I have included a glossary of terms associated with navajas and their use. The glossary was devised as an aid for readers who are conversant in the Spanish language as well as for those who are not.

The bilingual reader will note that many of the words in the original manual were spelled differently than they are today. The words *jitano, jiro, contrajiro,* and *jente* in the manual, for example, should actually be *gitano, giro, contragiro,* and *gente*. Similarly, *estravagante, ecsamen,* and *esplica* are found in the manual replacing *extravagante, examen,* and *explica*. Many other unconventional spellings are found throughout, and it is difficult to determine if all of them were the conventional spellings of the time or misspellings on the author's part. When creating this glossary, I kept the terms, misspelled or otherwise, as they appear in the original manual.

Time has a well-documented habit of influencing, redefining, and altering written and spoken languages, and Spanish is no exception. In some cases time extinguishes the use of certain words and phrases; at other times it has the more confounding effect of thoroughly changing their original meanings.

The terms below are defined strictly in accordance with their meanings in the context of the manual. The Spanish term appears on the left in boldface. The first definition that follows in English is the literal meaning. Any definitions or explanations after that refer to the term's meaning(s) in the context of the manual and the language of the *navajero* and/or *baratero*.

Abanico: Fan. *Navajero* slang for *navaja*.
Acero Sevillano: Sevillian steel; the informal name used to denote the knife-fighting systems of Andalusia.
Acometer: To attack aggressively or violently.
Alfiler: Sewing pin. *Navajero* slang for *navaja*.
Atracar: To attack. To deliver an aggressive blow to the opponent.
Baratero: One who, by one means or another, exacts a per-

centage from the winnings of gamblers. The percentage is known as the *barato*, hence the name *baratero*. The *baratero*, who was a member of the criminal underworld known as *la gente del hampa*, used his *navaja* to induce payment of the *barato* from gamblers.

Cambios: Changes (of hands). Foists, or the tactic of passing the knife from one hand to the other.

Cobrar el barato: Collect the commission. In return for his "work" in the gambling dens, the *baratero* earned an established percentage of the gamblers' bets and winnings. This percentage or cut was called the *barato*. Should any gamblers refuse to pay him his *barato*, the *baratero* could be expected to draw his *navaja* and either enforce payment or literally extract his payment in blood from his victim.

Contrajiro: Counterturn, properly spelled, *contragiro*. A defensive counterturn or counterpivot. A tactical response to an attempted *giro*. See also *jiro*.

Contrario: Adversary. In the manual, the *opponent* when describing the techniques of the *navaja*. See also *diestro*.

Corbatín de Vizcaya: Biscayan bowtie. A form of gallows. The Spanish term for the garrote as a method of execution. The garrote was the standard method of execution in Spain, first introduced in 1813 during the reign of Ferdinand II and used for civilians up until 1974. In its most typical application, the condemned was seated with his back to a post, and a rope or noose was looped around his or her neck. The ends of the rope were fed through the hole in the post. The executioner twisted a tourniquet handle inserted in the loop to tighten the rope and slowly tightened the noose about the condemned's neck until it was thoroughly crushed.

Corrida: A run or a chase. In the manual, the footwork used by opponents to circle and maneuver against one another during a knife fight.

Corte: Edge. *Navajero* slang for *navaja*.

Cuchillo: A fixed-blade knife. The subject of the third section of the manual.

Desafio: A challenge; an insult. An invitation to duel.

Desjarretazo: Term derived from the verb *desjarretar*, meaning to hamstring or to debilitate. *Navajero* slang for a ripping knife attack.

Destreza: Dexterity, skill, or adeptness. The Spanish style of fencing was traditionally referred to as *La Verdadera Arte de la Destreza*, or simply *Destreza*. The term was coined by Jeronimo de Carranza, founder of the Spanish school, in his definitive text on swordplay, *Libro Que Trata de la Filosofia de las Armas* (1583). The *Destreza* was later formalized by Carranza's disciple, Don Luis Pacheco de Narvaez, in his *Libro de las Grandezas de la Espada* (1600).

Diestro: A skilled individual; one who possesses skill and adroitness in an art or discipline. The *exponent* when describing the techniques of the *navaja*. See also *contrario*.

Enfilar: To line up or keep straight. *Navajero* slang for a thrust to the face.

Engaño: A deception; a ruse used to deceive the opponent.

Escuela aislada: Isolated school. In the manual, a term referring to any of the individualized styles of knife play practiced throughout Spain.

Espinazo: Vertebral column (slang).

Floretazo: A thrust made with a *florete*, or fencing foil. In the manual, a quick thrust with the *navaja* or *cuchillo*.

Florete: A fencing foil.

Fullero: A card sharper; one who prepares decks of marked cards.

Gente del hampa: The underworld; the criminal classes.

Germania: Language of the criminal underworld; thieves' slang.

Gitanería: Gypsy quarters.

Herramienta: Tool. *Navajero* slang for *navaja*.

Hierro: Iron tool. *Navajero* slang for *navaja*.

Huida: Flight. An evasive or retreating movement in knife combat.

Jácaro: A ruffian; one poised to disappear with the money (gambling wagers).

Jiro: Pivot, turn, or rotation, properly spelled, *giro*. A pivoting turn used to gain—and to attack from—the opponent's flanks. The noun *giro* derives from the verb *girar*, to pivot, turn, or rotate. See also *contrajiro*.

Jitanos: Spanish term for Gypsies, properly spelled *Gitanos*. Spanish Gypsies refer to themselves as *Calés*, or *Gaches*.

Molinete: Small windmill. A technique where one lifts one foot off the ground and pivots on the other while extending the knife and delivering a thrust at the attacker. Also known as a *cuadrada*.

Mojá: Andalusian contraction for *mojada*, or wet blow (i.e., a blow that draws blood).

Navaja: Traditional Spanish clasp knife. *Navajas* were characterized by the clasp or ring that was pulled to release the open blade and fold it into the handle.

Palmo: The span of one hand. Used as a standard of measure.

Parte alta: Upper part. The high line; anatomical targets located from waist to the forehead.

Parte baja: Lower part. The low line; anatomical targets located from the waist to the feet.

Planta: Stance. A guard position in knife combat. See also *Posicion*,

Posicion: Position or stance. A guard position.

Pregonero: A tout.

Pícaro: A rogue.

Pincho: Prick (conventional sense). *Navajero* slang for *navaja*.

Plumada: *Navajero* slang for a forehand slash.

Puñal: Dagger.

Puñalá: Andalusian contraction for *puñalada*, or knife thrust.

Quite: A parry.

Recortes: An evasive movement performed with the entire body. Resembles a *jiro* used to retreat.

Recursos: Recourses. In the manual, and in the time and jargon of the *baratero*, an expedient recourse or tactic of last resort.

Revés: Reverse. *Navajero* term for a backhand slash.

Rufo: A bully.

Santólio: Contraction of *santo olio*, or "holy oil." A large *navaja*.

Sevillana: Feminine adjective meaning "Sevillian." A *navaja* with formidable point and edge qualities, specifically designed for combat.

Suerte: Luck (in modern Spanish). In the manual, and in the time and jargon of the *baratero*, a tactic.

Suerte de la Culebra: Tactic of the snake. A technique where the *navajero* drops to the ground and strikes the opponent in the lower half of the body. The tactic appears to resemble the classic *pasatta sotto*.

Terreno: Ground, terrain. "Boundary," however, best captures the author's intended meaning.

Treta: Feint in the vernacular of fencing. In the manual, the term is intended to denote a ruse, trick, or tactic used to gain an advantage in combat. Similar to the term *suerte*.

Tijeras: Scissors. The term, however, is a misnomer. Gypsies typically worked as *esquiladores*, or horse grooms and, as a tool of this trade, generally carried a pair of mule shears in a sheath on their belt. These shears—not scissors—were actually called *cachas* in caló, the dialect of the Spanish Gypsy.

Vagabundos: Vagabonds or vagrants; able-bodied persons who shunned respectable jobs: members of the criminal underclass.

Viaje: Journey or voyage. *Navajero* slang for a low-line thrust to the belly.

The *Baratero*-Based Syllabus

As already mentioned, the topics of the lessons in *Manual del Baratero* represent important aspects of combat that are as relevant today as when the work was originally written. Though much of the "instruction" contained in the manual deserves sober scrutiny, many *navaja* aficionados nonetheless use the list of topics as a yardstick by which to measure the completeness of their own personal methods. To illustrate how they accomplish this, one such syllabus is included here as a guideline for the interested reader.

Note that while several topics are redundantly addressed at various points throughout the manual, we have listed such topics only once and in the sequence we believe makes the most sense. Remember also that the historical *barateros'* techniques are decidedly elementary in comparison to how the *navaja* is actually wielded in *contemporary* circles. As such, the *barateros'* techniques represent the most basic of *navaja* techniques and serve only as a starting point for understanding the core of the art of knife fighting.

SAMPLE SYLLABUS

I. FUNDAMENTALS
A. Background
1. History (precedence, fencing influences, bullfighting influences, etc.)
2. Weapons (swords, fixed-blade knives, folding knives, scissors)
3. Terms for the *navaja* (regional terms, class-specific terms, etc.)

B. Knife-handling Essentials
1. Grips
2. Positions, stances, and guards

C. Boundaries and Proper Combat Distance
1. Weapon length
2. Arm reach
3. Footwork and mobility

D. Attacks
1. *Puñalada*
2. *Enfilada*
3. *Viaje*
4. *Tajo*
5. *Desjarretazo*
6. Others (e.g., *atravesada, metisaca, puntazo*)

E. Defenses
1. Parries
2. Evasions, leaps

F. Footwork
1. Advance
2. Retreat
3. Body shifts
4. Pivots
5. Counterpivots
6. *Corridas*

G. Targets
1. High line
2. Low line

3. Inside line
4. Outside line

II. SPECIFIC TECHNIQUES
  A. Foists
  B. Counterthrusts
    1. *Molinete*
    2. *Floretazo*
  C. Uses of the Off Hand
    1. Empty
    2. Hat
    3. Sash
    4. Cape/cloak, jacket
  D. Throwing the *Navaja*

III. TECHNIQUE OVERLAP
  A. *Cuchillo* (slashing, thrusting, striking, etc.)
  B. *Navaja* (slashing, thrusting, etc.)
  C. *Puñal* (thrusting, throwing, etc.)
  D. *Tijeras* (thrusting, throwing, etc.)
  E. Empty Hands (slash counters, thrust counters, throw counters)

IV. SKILL DEVELOPMENT
  A. Grip Changes and Dexterity Drills
  B. *Corridas* (maintaining distance and bridging the gap)
  C. *Quites* and *Huidas* (tactical applications of parries and evasions)
  D. *Recursos* and *Tretas* (strategies, tactics, feints, tricks, ruses)

These topics represent a core curriculum that can be modified, reduced, or expanded upon, depending on the reader's personal and stylistic preferences. The topics derive from those found in *Manual del Baratero*, but their application and execution must conform to the limits of what is practical.

Practicing fanciful or over stylized techniques is not only a waste of training time and effort but is actually detrimental if and when such techniques are used in place of more appropriate combative responses. As the late Santiago Rivera was fond of saying, "It is better to avoid such techniques in the same manner that an ugly woman avoids a photographer."

Partial List of
Other Works by M.d.R.

Celnart, Madama. *Manual Completo de Juegos de Sociedad, o Tertulia y de Prendas.* Translated from French by Mariano de Rementeria y Fica. Imprenta de Palacios, Madrid, 1831.

Conferencias Gramaticales Sobre La Lengua Castellana, o Elementos Esplanados de Ella. Mariano de Rementeria y Fica, ed. Imprenta de Fuentenebro, Madrid, 1843.

El Hombre Fino al Gusto del Día, o Manual de Urbanidad, Cortesía y Buen Tono. Translated from French by Mariano de Rementeria y Fica. Imprenta de Moreno, Madrid, 1830.

Manual del Cocinero, Cocinera y Repostero, con Un Tratado de Confitería y Botillería. Translated from French by Mariano de Rementeria y Fica. Imprenta de D.L. Amarita, 1828.

Vergani, M.A. *Gramática Italiana Simplificada y Reducida a 20 Lecciones.* Translated from Italian by Mariano de Rementeria y Fica, 1826.

Bibliography

Amberger, J. Christoph. *The Secret History of the Sword.*
 Burbank, Calif.: Unique Publications, 1999.
Appletons' Journal: A Magazine of General Literature 11, 267
 (May 2, 1874).

Borrow, George Henry. *Zincali: An Account of the Gypsies in Spain*. New York: Wiley & Putnam, 1899.

Cassidy, William. *The Complete Book of Knife Fighting*. Boulder, Colo.: Paladin Press, 1975.

D'Avillier, Charles, and Gustave Doré. *Spain*. London: Sampson, Marston, Searle & Rivington, 1881.

De Brea, Antonio Manuel. *Principios de Destreza del Espadín*. Madrid: Imprenta Real, 1805.

Defourneaux, Marcelin. *Daily Life in Spain in the Golden Age*. Translated by Newton Branch. Palo Alto, Calif.: Stanford University Press, 1979.

Depetris, Jose Carlos. *El Duelo Criollo*. http://pampapalabra.freeservers.com/aaduelo.htm (accessed October 6, 2004).

Gallichan, Walter M. *The Story of Seville*. London: J.M. Dent & Co., 1903.

Gautier, Théophile. *Voyage en Espagne*. Paris: Charpentier, 1843.

Gracián, Baltasar. *El Arte de la Prudencia (The Art of Worldly Wisdom)*. Huesca, Spain: Juan Nogues, 1647.

Grant, Bruce. *The Cowboy Encyclopedia*. New York: Rand McNally & Co., 1951.

Levine, Bernard. *Pocket Knives*. Edison, N.J.: Chartwell Books, 1998.

Loriega, James. *Sevillian Steel: The Traditional Knife-Fighting Arts of Spain*. Boulder, Colo.: Paladin Press, 1999.

Martinez, Ramón, and Jeannette Acosta-Martinez. *La Verdadera Destreza: The True Art and Skill of Spanish Swordsmanship*, Vols. 1 and 2. Hollywood, Calif.: Palpable Hit Productions, 2002.

Martínez del Peral, Rafael. *La Navaja Española Antigua*. Madrid: Sietefam. S.L., 1995.

Mérimée, Prosper. *Carmen*. Translated by Lady Mary Lloyd. New York: P.F. Collier & Son, 1901.

Ocete Rubio, Rafael. *Armas Blancas en España*. Madrid: Edimat Libros S.A., 1984.

Perry, Mary Elizabeth. *Crime and Society in Early Modern Seville.* Hanover, N.H.: Dartmouth University Press, 1980.

Peterson, Harold L. *Daggers and Fighting Knives of the Western World.* New York: Walker & Company, 1968.

Pike, Ruth. *Aristocrats and Traders: Sevillian Society in the Sixteenth Century.* Ithaca, New York: Cornell University Press, 1972.

Rousseau, Jean-Jacques. *La Nouvelle Heloise.* Translated by Judith McDowell. University Park, Pa.: Pennsylvania State University Press, 1987.

Sanchez de Vivar, Arturo. *La Navaja Clásica.* Madrid: Aldaba Ediciones S.A., 1991

Smith, Collin. *Diccionario Español-Inglés, Inglés-Español,* 5ta ed. Barcelona: Grijalbo Mondadori S.A., 1999.

About the Translator

James Loriega began his formal edged-weapons training in 1967 when he embarked on a lifelong study of martial arts with Ronald Duncan, the "father of American ninjutsu."

In the mid-1970s, after achieving various instructor-level ranks in Asian systems, Loriega gained his first exposure to the Western martial traditions under the tutelage of Maître Michel Alaux, a former coach to the U.S. Olympic Fencing Team. It was from Maître Alaux, and his assistant at the time, Ms. Julia Jones, that Loriega learned the rudiments of épée and saber.

In September 1980, Loriega founded the New York Ninpokai, the city's premier training academy for the traditional arts of ninjutsu. In 1990, while conducting ninjutsu seminars in Spain, Loriega discovered the *acero sevillano* knife arts of Andalusia. These arts include the use of the *cuchillo* (knife), *puñal* (stiletto), *bastón de estoque* (sword cane), *bastón de paseo* (walking stick), and *navaja* (clasp

Loriega inspecting a *sevillana.*

MANUAL OF THE *BARATERO*

knife). From 1991 to 1996 he spent his summers in Seville learning the intricacies of these Andalusian arts.

In August 1996, Loriega received certification as an *instructor de Armas Blancas Sevillanas* under *Maestro de Armas* Santiago Rivera, then headmaster of the *Escuela Sevillana de Armas Blancas.* At this time he also completed his first translation of *Manual del Baratero.*

Since 1996, Loriega has operated a recognized branch of the *Escuela Sevillana* in New York City known as the Raven Arts Institute.

In September 2000, following the publication of *Sevillian Steel: The Traditional Knife-Fighting Arts of Spain* (Paladin Press, 1999), Loriega was formally acknowledged as a *maestro de Armas Blancas Sevillanas.*

In January 2002, Loriega was inducted to the International Masters-at-Arms Federation (IMAF), where he is recognized for his mastery of the *navaja* and other Andalusian edged weapons. Based in Milan, Italy, the IMAF states that its mission is "to preserve, study, practice, and teach the martial arts of the Western world heritage [and] to function as a guild of professional teachers in keeping with the tradition and heritage of arms."

Loriega's extensive writings have appeared in mainstream martial arts publications such as *Black Belt, Warriors, Ninja,* and *Tactical Knives.* His first book, *Sevillian Steel,* presents an overview of the edged weapons culture, styles, and strategies of this Western martial tradition.

A second book, *Scourge of the Dark Continent* (Loompanics, 1999), outlines the history and martial applications of the African *sjambok* (a rodlike whip made from rhinoceros hide). Following the release of the present annotated English-language translation of the 19th century *Manual del Baratero,* he will publish the sequel to *Sevillian Steel,* detailing the technical intricacies of using the *navaja.*

Loriega continues to travel and to train, in addition to offering instruction at the Raven Arts Institute, where courses are available in the use of the folding knife, stiletto, sword-

cane, walking stick, improvised weaponry, and unarmed com-
batives. Serious inquiries may be addressed to him at

Raven Arts Institute of Sevillian Steel
2620 East 18th Street
Brooklyn, NY 11235